The Speech-Language Pathologist's Guide to Dyslexia

Courtney Overton, Jeannette Roberes, Danelle Augustine, DeJunné Clark Jackson, Dr. Lauren McClenney-Rosenstein, Christina Pompeo, & Brittany Zucker

Foreword by Dr. Tiffany P. Hogan

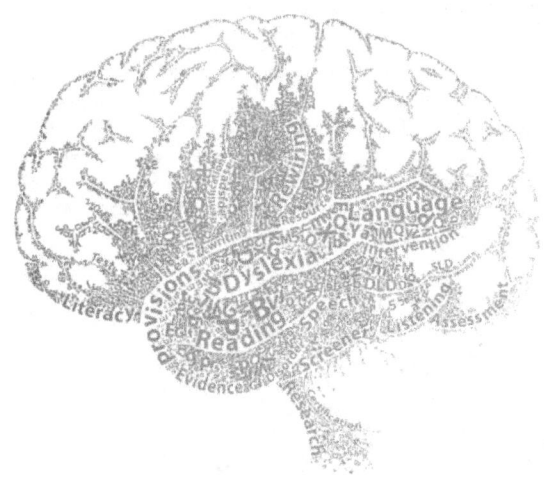

SLP Publishing House

Alexandria, Virginia

THE SPEECH-LANGUAGE PATHOLOGIST'S GUIDE TO DYSLEXIA

Paperback ISBN: 979-8-218-09555-0

Ebook ISBN: 979-8-218-09556-7

Printed in the United States of America

Cover by Karen Captline, BetterBe Creative

Edited by Cori Wamsley, Aurora Corialis Publishing

Praise

The *Speech-Language Pathologist's Guide to Dyslexia* provides a well-informed and accessible guide to understanding the essential role speech-language pathologists (SLPs) play in early identification and intervention for dyslexia. Given the high incidence of developmental language disorders in individuals with dyslexia, SLPs are often the first specialists supporting children at risk for reading difficulties. As experts in typical speech and language development, SLPs are uniquely positioned to identify risk factors and begin the early intervention essential for maximizing client outcomes.

Not all SLP training, however, delves deeply into the inextricable relationship between spoken and written language. With their many years of experience, the authors fill that knowledge gap for you.

Through the expert lenses of these SLPs and educators, you will learn the necessary skills to spot the early signs of dyslexia, assess individuals, and plan evidence-based intervention. You will feel equipped to advocate for clients after reading the authors' summary of the most pertinent research and their guide to state dyslexia laws. In addition, the authors present an accessible discussion and illustrations that will support you in explaining the brain basis of language and reading challenges.

This book will become a much-used resource for SLPs to assist in early identification and intervention, to advocate for clients with dyslexia, and to explain the critical role of the SLP in assessing and supporting all individuals with reading and writing challenges.

Trish Kelley-Nazzaro, MS, CCC-SLP

Program Director, Certificate of Advanced Study in Literacy and Language

Assistant Professor, Department of Communication Sciences and Disorders

MGH Institute of Health Professions

Table of Contents

Foreword

By Tiffany P. Hogan, PhD, CCC-SLP, FASHA

"A journey of a thousand miles begins with a single step."

—Lao Tzu

Dyslexia is a neurobiological brain-based difference that makes it difficult to accurately and fluently read and spell words (IDA, n.d.). It is a language-based learning disability in which the form of language—phonology—is most affected (Hogan, 2022). Across the lifespan, difficulty processing the phonological aspects of language results in trouble producing speech sounds, remembering letter(s)-sound(s) correspondences, learning new words, remembering auditorily presented information, and following directions (Catts & Kamhi, 2012). In addition, the majority of children with dyslexia—50–80%—have a co-occurring developmental language disorder (DLD) (Adlof & Hogan, 2018). DLD involves difficulty using and understanding language, especially the content of language—vocabulary and grammar (McGregor et al., 2020). As a result of their difficulties, children with dyslexia, with or without DLD, tend to read fewer texts, which puts them at risk for academic failure and other negative life outcomes (Duff et al., 2014).

Children with speech and language impairments are at least 6 times more likely to have reading problems (Stoeckel et al., 2013). Simply stated, children on your caseload are children with dyslexia (Komesidou & Hogan, 2020). As such, speech-language pathologists (SLPs) are in a unique position to advocate because you are often the first professional to support a child with dyslexia, even before their dyslexia manifests. SLPs are also uniquely equipped to support reading skills as experts in language development (both language form and content), diagnostic assessment, and personalized interventions (ASHA, 2001). As a clinical speech-language pathologist (SLP) and researcher for over 20 years, I have worked with and studied children with dyslexia, their families, and the professionals who support them. One resounding fact is clear to me, study after study and in my vast clinical experience: SLPs can make significant positive impacts on the lives of children and adults with dyslexia (Hogan, 2018), and the earlier they do so, the better the child's long-term outcome (Catts & Hogan, 2021).

Unfortunately, though, many SLPs have limited training in dyslexia and even more limited opportunities for training due to large caseloads and stretched resources. Enter this fantastic book! The authors have provided an invaluable resource that every SLP should own. They provide research-based factual information through a clinically relevant, practical lens in bite-size, easy-to-read chapters. They do so while covering an impressive breadth and depth of information from the brain basis of dyslexia to state laws to assessment procedures to evidence-based interventions.

Whether you have extensive knowledge of dyslexia, very little, or anywhere in between, this book is for you. Packed with useful materials and resources, after reading this small but mighty book, SLPs will have a strong foundation to better support the children they serve, more confidently contribute to literacy initiatives, and continue to learn more about children with dyslexia.

References

Adlof, S.M. & Hogan, T.P. (2018). Understanding dyslexia in the context of developmental language disorders. *Language, Speech, and Hearing Services in Schools, 49,* 762-773.

American Speech-Language-Hearing Association. (2001). *Roles and responsibilities of speech-language pathologists with respect to reading and writing in children and adolescents* [Position Statement]. Retrieved from www.asha.org/policy.

Catts, H.W. & Hogan, T.P. (2021). Dyslexia: An ounce of prevention is better than a pound of diagnosis and treatment. *The Reading League Journal, 2,* 6-13.

Catts, H.W. & Kamhi, A.G. (2012). *Language and Reading Disabilities,* 3rd Edition. Pearson.

Duff, D., Tomblin, J. B., & Catts, H. (2015). The influence of reading on vocabulary growth: A case for a Matthew effect. *Journal of Speech, Language, and Hearing Research, 58*(3), 853-864.

Hogan, T.P. (2018). Five ways speech-language pathologists can positively impact children with dyslexia. *Language, Speech, and Hearing Services in Schools, 49*, 902-905.

Hogan, T.P. (2022). What's language got to do with it? Speech-language pathology contributions to the science of reading. In press in *The Reading League Journal.*

International Dyslexia Association. (n.d.). *Dyslexia Assessment: What Is It and How Can It Help?* [Fact Sheet]. Retrieved from https://dyslexiaida.org/dyslexia-assessment-what-is-it-and-how-can-it-help-2/

Komesidou, R. & Hogan. T.P. (2020). Preschool language precursors to later reading problems. *Perspectives on Language and Literacy, 46*, 37-41.

McGregor, K. K., Goffman, L., Van Horne, A.O., Hogan, T.P., & Finestack, L.H. (2020). Developmental language disorder: Applications for advocacy, research and clinical service. *Perspectives of the ASHA Special Interest Group, SIG 1 Language Learning and Education.*

Stoeckel, R. E., Colligan, R. C., Barbaresi, W. J., Weaver, A. L., Killian, J. M., & Katusic, S. K. (2013). Early speech-language impairment and risk for written language disorder: A population-based study. *Journal of developmental and behavioral pediatrics: JDBP, 34*(1), 38.

Biography

Tiffany P. Hogan, PhD, CCC-SLP, FASHA, is a professor in the Department of Communication Sciences and Disorders at MGH Institute of Health Professions in Boston, director of the Speech and Language (SAiL) Literacy Lab, and research associate at Harvard University. Dr. Hogan has published over 100 papers on the genetic, neurologic, and behavioral links between oral and written language development, with a focus on improving assessment and intervention for children with developmental language disorder, dyslexia, and/or speech sound disorders. Her advocacy for children with reading difficulties has led her to co-found a DLD informational website: www.dldandme.org, host a podcast, SeeHearSpeak Podcast (www.seehearspeakpodcast.com), and contribute information for articles in numerous news outlets including *The New York Times* and *The Boston Globe*, along with several television and radio appearances. Follow her on twitter @tiffanyphogan, Instagram @seehearspeakpodcast, and Facebook @sailliteracylab. Email: thogan@mghihp.edu

The Speech-Language Pathologist's Guide to Dyslexia

American Speech-Language-Hearing Association Position Statement

Roles and Responsibilities of Speech-Language Pathologists With Respect to Reading and Writing in Children and Adolescents

Ad Hoc Committee on Reading and Written Language Disorders

About this Document

This position statement, guidelines, and technical report were drafted by an ad hoc committee formed by the American Speech-Language-Hearing Association (ASHA). Members of the Ad Hoc Committee on Reading and Written Language Disorders were Nickola Wolf Nelson (chair), Hugh Catts, Barbara J. Ehren, Froma P. Roth, Cheryl M. Scott, and Maureen Staskowski. Vice Presidents for Professional Practices in Speech-Language Pathology Nancy Creaghead (1997–1999) and Alex Johnson (2000–2002) provided guidance and support. Roseanne P. Clausen provided ex officio assistance from the National Office; Diane Paul-Brown and Susan Karr served as consultants to the committee.

Position Statement

It is the position of the American Speech-Language-Hearing Association (ASHA) that speech-language pathologists (SLPs) play a critical and direct role in the development of literacy for children and adolescents with communication disorders, [1] including those with severe or multiple disabilities. SLPs also make a contribution to the literacy efforts of a school district or community on behalf of other children and adolescents. These roles are implemented in collaboration with others who have expertise in the development of written language and vary with settings and experience of those involved. [2]

The connections between spoken and written language are well established in that (a) spoken language provides the foundation for the development of reading and writing; (b) spoken and written language have a reciprocal relationship, such that each builds on the other to result in general language and literacy competence, starting early and continuing through childhood into adulthood; (c) children with spoken language problems frequently have difficulty learning to read and write, and children with reading and writing problems frequently have difficulty with spoken language [3] ; and (d) instruction in spoken language can result in growth in written language, and instruction in written language can result in growth in spoken language.

As with difficulty in learning to listen and speak, difficulty in learning to read and write can involve any of the components of language—phonology, morphology, syntax, semantics, and pragmatics. Problems can occur in the production, comprehension, and awareness of language at the sound, syllable, word, sentence, and discourse levels. Individuals with reading and writing problems also may experience difficulties in using language strategically to communicate, think, and learn. These fundamental connections necessitate that intervention for language disorders target written as well as spoken language needs.

SLPs' knowledge of normal and disordered language acquisition, and their clinical experience in developing individualized programs for children and adolescents, prepare them to assume a variety of roles related to the development of reading and writing. Appropriate roles and responsibilities for SLPs include, but are not limited to (a) preventing written language problems by fostering language acquisition and emergent literacy; (b) identifying children at risk for reading and writing problems; (c) assessing reading and writing; (d) providing intervention and documenting outcomes for reading and writing; and (e) assuming other roles, such as providing assistance to general education teachers, parents, and students; advocating for effective literacy practices; and advancing the knowledge base. These roles are dynamic in relation to the evolving knowledge base and have implications for research and professional education.

Notes

[1] The scope of practice for SLPs includes literacy assessment and intervention for adults (with developmental or acquired communication disorders) as well as for children and adolescents, but that work is beyond the scope of this set of papers.

[2] The term written language refers to reading and writing and related processes.

[3] In these documents, the terms problems, difficulties, and impairments are used interchangeably to describe concerns about spoken or written language development; where applicable, literature reviews maintain terminology of the original.

doi:10.1044/policy.PS2001-00104

Reference

American Speech-Language-Hearing Association. (2001). *Roles and responsibilities of speech-language pathologists with respect to reading and writing in children and adolescents* [Position Statement]. Retrieved from www.asha.org/policy.

Chapter 1
History of Dyslexia

By DeJunné Clark Jackson, MA, MAT, MEd,
CALT, LDT

*"Being misidentified can be just as detrimental as not
being identified at all."*

What if I told you that there was a way to prevent reading failures, assist in closing academic learning gaps, and change students' trajectories in life? Would I have your attention? You'd probably scream from the rooftops, "SIGN ME UP!" Well, as a teacher-mama, I thought I was doing just that. Unfortunately, I have had a front row seat far too many times to the learning challenges of students—my own included.

I began to see some difficulty in my child's learning process as he began his school journey. After a long and arduous process, we uncovered his dyslexia. From then on, I stepped out on a mission to help not only my child but all the other struggling kids in schools. As a school counselor for several years, I facilitated a broken system of "help" for students daily. On any given day, during parent-teacher conferences and team meetings, I sat cringing in my seat—frustrated, perplexed, and bewildered. How was it that so many educators were unaware of dyslexia? So, here I am! Creating well-informed educational environments that empower educators and practitioners. By engaging in this topic, we can have an immense impact on students.

Dyslexia has a long history of both existence and controversy. The word "dyslexia" derives from the Greek word parts *dys* (meaning "difficulty") and *lex* (meaning "words"). As defined today by the National Institute of Neurological Disorders and Stroke (NINDS):

> Dyslexia is a brain-based type of learning disability that specifically impairs a person's ability to read. These individuals typically read at levels significantly lower than expected despite having normal intelligence. Although the disorder varies from person to person, common characteristics among people with dyslexia are difficulty with **phonological processing** (the manipulation of sounds), spelling, and/or rapid visual-verbal responding. In individuals with adult onset of dyslexia, it usually occurs as a result of brain injury or in the context of dementia; this contrasts with individuals with dyslexia who simply were never identified as children or adolescents. Dyslexia can be inherited in some families, and recent studies have identified a number of genes that may predispose an individual to developing dyslexia.

In the context of a working definition of dyslexia most often used for diagnosis, it is a **specific learning disability** associated with specific deficits in reading skills based on cognitive functioning. The deficits manifest through difficulties with fluent word reading and recognition, spelling, and **decoding**. Additionally, the phonological component of language is impacted, which can affect reading comprehension and an overall reduced reading experience (Lyon, Shaywitz, & Shaywitz, 2003, p. 2). When defining dyslexia and its relevance to the speech therapy practitioners, Kamhi & Catts (2005) recalls that there is a long historical basis for reading disabilities. Acknowledging the importance of perspective, they noted that regardless of the focus on learning disabilities, reading disabilities, perceptual-motor or visual correlations of such, the story begins with the core fact that language factors are critical in the disability.

Here, we will journey through the history and origins of dyslexia. Dyslexia, as an evolving and concrete yet abstract disability, has roots that go back as early as 1676 when the German physician Dr. Johann Schmidt published observations of a sixty-five-year-old man who lost reading ability following a stroke. This was termed "acquired alexia." Then in 1877, Adolf Kussmaul, a German neurologist, coined the term "word-blindness" which was largely due to the 1872 publishing from British neurologist Sir William Broadbent. Broadbent reported on a patient who could see the words but was not able to understand them. Dr. W. Pringle Morgan of Seaford wrote in 1896 about a patient with reading difficulty but bright and intelligent otherwise.

In the U.S., the first reported case of childhood reading difficulty came in 1905 from a Cleveland ophthalmologist, Dr. W. E. Bruner. In the 1920s, Dr. Samuel T. Orton, a pathologist & neurologist, became known as the "Father of Dyslexia" for his work with strephosymbolia (or twisted symbols). Orton identified the syndrome of specific language disability. He separated disabled readers from students with mental disability, brain damage, and primary emotional disturbances. Dr. Orton also proposed a system for diagnosis and outlined the principles of remediation for disabled readers. Along with Anna Gillingham, psychologist and teacher, they analyzed and organized the English language for the teaching procedures that Dr. Orton devised (1930s). Dr. Gillingham trained teachers in this multisensory method.

The Orton-Gillingham method utilized an approach to teach reading for children with dyslexia that was a sequential, alphabetic-phonetic multi-sensory program. The approach called for the intentional instruction of the English language. Fast forward to 1987, when the U.S. Congress mandated that federal research priorities be investigated with regard to learning disabilities.

This abbreviated timeline just touches on the evolution of and continuing research into dyslexia. The most recent federal definition for dyslexia is associated with adult illiteracy, specifically in the prison system. The First Step Act of 2018, a recidivism reduction program, called for the screening of all prison inmates for characteristics of dyslexia. In a 2000 Texas prison study, 80% of inmates were found to be functionally illiterate, which was found to be associated with their sustainability outside of the prison system.

A plethora of scientific studies and research support the existence of dyslexia in some form for centuries. This rich history has helped to develop the practical applications suggested by practitioners to address dyslexia as a learning disability. Through this history, dyslexia is explained and explored from a cognitive level and a neurobiological base, exploring the brain and its mechanics. Functional Magnetic Resonance Imaging (fMRI) was utilized in studies in 1996 as a method to image the brain to discover how oxygenated blood flowed when participants were given a series of words to distinguish their rhyming correlation. This scan was fundamental in utilizing science and technology to concretely aid in the diagnosis of dyslexia—activating neurons in the Broca area of the brain. Through their brain images, the study gave all participants a sense of self and helped them see how their brain functioned differently yet was "normal" in its design.

Looking at current practices, many areas of teaching reading resulted from the history and research of dyslexia. One, most notable, is the science of reading movement. This movement derived from years of poor reading outcomes for children, as a result of the reading wars—distinguishing itself from methods of teaching reading based on balanced literacy or whole language approaches. While those approaches encouraged habits such as guessing words, using picture clues, and rote memorization of words, the science of reading promotes systematic, explicit instruction of literacy skills based on the way our brains acquire those skills.

According to *The Science of Reading: A Defining Movement* (2021):

> The science of reading is a vast, interdisciplinary body of *scientifically based research* about reading and issues related to reading and writing. This research has been conducted over the last five decades across the world, and it is derived from thousands of studies conducted in multiple languages. The science of reading has culminated in a preponderance of evidence to inform how proficient reading and writing develop; why some have difficulty; and how we can most effectively assess and teach and, therefore, improve student outcomes through prevention of and intervention for reading difficulties. The science of reading is derived from researchers from multiple fields: cognitive psychology, communication sciences, developmental psychology, education, special education, implementation science, linguistics, and neuroscience.

The important distinction between the science of reading and the history of dyslexia remains in the robust evolution of centuries of evidence related to diagnosing, treating, and remediating dyslexic individuals, which is the catalyst for science of reading research.

Like many aspects of the education system, dyslexia remains controversial in its universal definition, identification, prevalence, and equitable application. Psychologists, neurologists, psychiatrists, pediatricians, educators, parents, sociologists, and economists all can be invested in getting this right for the sake of children and adults alike. Since the earliest research, there is evidence of children struggling to read in spite of appropriate classroom instruction. Reading development is a technical process that, in the absence of dyslexia, can be a magical and profoundly enjoyable experience.

Timeline

- 1676 — German physician, Dr. Johann Schmidt, termed "acquired alexia"
- 1877 — Adolf Kussmaul, a German neurologist, coined the term "word-blindness"
- 1887 — "Dyslexia" first used by Dr. Rudolf Berlin, a German ophthalmologist
- 1896 — Dr. W. Pringle Morgan of Seaford wrote about a patient with reading difficulty but bright and intelligent otherwise
- 1905 — In the U.S., Cleveland ophthalmologist, Dr. W. E. Bruner, first reported case of childhood reading difficulty
- 1926 — Samuel T. Orton, pathologist, and neurologist, known as the father of dyslexia; presented *Interpretation of Developmental Reading Disability to The American Neurological Association*

- 1987 — U.S. Congress mandated that federal research priorities be investigated with regard to learning disabilities
- 1996 — First fMRI brain mapping, without use of radioactive tracers, to study the brain's role in reading and a means to view how the brain reads
- 2018 — The First Step Act, federal legislation addressing prison literacy, offers additional dyslexia definition
- 2021 — *The Science of Reading: A Defining Movement* was published

Biography

DeJunné Clark Jackson, MA, MAT, MEd, CALT, LDT is an educational professional with over a decade of experience in the roles of a university disabilities coordinator, classroom teacher, school counselor, student services coordinator, and reading interventionist. As the parent of a child with dyslexia, DeJunné is on a mission to spread awareness to parents and schools and advocate for appropriate remediation needs within the school setting and fair treatment of and the appropriate access to literacy education for all children.

DeJunné currently serves as the vice president of program development at The Center for Literacy & Learning. Prior to joining the team, DeJunné was actively and fiercely operating Learning Fundamentals Educational Therapy & Consulting, a private practice, specialized in aiding parents through the process of seeking school-based solutions for struggling learners. She holds a B.A. in political science and sociology, an M.A. in counseling and guidance, an M.A.T. in teaching, certified in pre-K-third grade, and an M.Ed. in dyslexia therapy. DeJunné is a certified academic language therapist, a licensed dyslexia therapist, and only one of three credentialed Association of Educational Therapists in Louisiana. She is a member of the Louisiana Department of Education's Early Literacy Commission, a state leader with Decoding Dyslexia Louisiana, and the current president of The Reading League Louisiana. Social Media: @DCJacksonTeach

References

Shaywitz, S. E. (2003). *Overcoming dyslexia: A new and complete science-based program for reading problems at any level*. New York: A.A. Knopf.

Lyon, G.R., Shaywitz, S.E., & Shaywitz, B.A. (2003). A definition of dyslexia. *Annals of Dyslexia*, 53, 1–14.

Birsh, J. R. (2011). *Multisensory teaching of basic language skills*. Baltimore: Paul H. Brookes Pub. Co.

Anderson, P. L. & Meier-Hedde, R. (2001). Early case reports of dyslexia in the United States and Europe. *Journal of Learning Disabilities*, 34 (1), 9–21.

Hinshelwood, J. (1896, November 21). A case of dyslexia: A peculiar form of word-blindness. *The Lancet*, 1451–1454.

Eden, G. F., VanMeter, J. W., Rumsey, J. M., Maisog, J. M., Woods, R. P., & Zeffiro, T. A. (1996). *Abnormal processing of visual motion in dyslexia revealed by functional brain imaging. Nature, 382*(6586), 66–69. doi:10.1038/382066a0.

Chapter 2
Neurological Underpinnings

By Brittany Zucker M.S. CCC-SLP, TSSLD, C-SLDI, A/OGA

"The best teachers remain students all their lives."

- John Stott

After receiving my master's degree in speech-language pathology, I worked at an elementary school in Harlem, New York, where most of my students were struggling to read. The school utilized the Balanced Literacy approach and encouraged students to guess on the first word, use pictures to decode, and focus on memorizing words. As a speech-language pathologist (SLP) who did not have a full understanding of dyslexia or Structured Literacy, I naively reinforced many of these strategies in my own speech and language sessions while continuously questioning why my students weren't progressing. Years later, as I embarked on my own personal education journey, I learned the science behind how the brain learns to read and finally understood the reason.

Introduction

Although dyslexia is a hidden disability, functional magnetic resonance imaging (fMRI) studies have provided evidence that reading difficulties are neurobiological in origin. With such advances in neuroscience, scientists are able to watch the neural systems of the brain at work as individuals read. These images have not only revealed that dyslexia has roots in the brain, but that there are also structural and functional differences between a proficient reader's brain and the brain of a struggling reader. Even though researchers have learned a lot about dyslexia and the brain, it is important to note that scientists are still unsure which brain differences cause dyslexia and which ones are caused by it.

Our Brains Aren't Hardwired to Read

Reading is a manmade skill. Our brains aren't hardwired to learn to read, so there is no reading center or one specific part of the brain we use for reading. Instead, reading involves processes that take place in different areas of the brain already in place for language and visual processing. When a child begins to learn the letters and their sounds and starts to decode written language, brain regions that serve other functions, such as spoken language and object recognition, are reorganized and connected. However, not all brains create a flowing circuit easily, which is why some individuals struggle to read.

Brain Anatomy

The brain is divided into two halves with different cognitive functions taking place in the right and left hemispheres. Connecting the left and right hemispheres is the corpus callosum, which carries messages from one hemisphere to the other. While the left hemisphere is important for language and logical processing, the right hemisphere is important for spatial perception. Each hemisphere is divided into four sections: frontal, parietal, temporal, and occipital. The cerebellum, which is located beneath the occipital lobes, controls movement and coordination. The functions of each brain region are summarized in the chart below.

Brain Region	Function
Frontal Lobe	This area is associated with executive functions, motor performance, and speech production. The frontal lobe makes it possible to understand simple and complex grammar. Broca's area, which is located here, plans the process of speech.
Parietal Lobe	Integrates sensory information
Temporal Lobe	Processes auditory information and contains the memory center of the brain. This area is responsible for

	phonological awareness and discriminating speech sounds. Wernicke's area, which is involved in comprehension of language, is located here.
Occipital Lobe	The visual processing center of the brain
Cerebellum	Responsible for maintaining balance, posture, and coordination of the body
Corpus Callosum	A large bundle of more than 200 million nerve fibers that connect the two brain hemispheres, which allows communication between the left and right sides of the brain
Brain Stem	Structure that connects the cerebrum of the brain to the spinal cord and cerebellum. It is responsible for regulating most of the body's automatic functions such as breathing and maintaining your heartbeat.

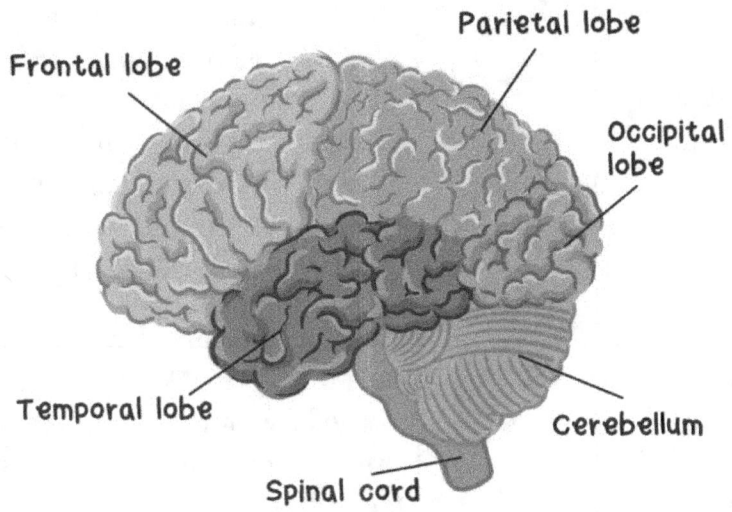

Human Brain Anatomy

Parietal lobe

Frontal lobe

Occipital lobe

Temporal lobe

Cerebellum

Spinal cord

The Reading Brain

While different regions of the brain serve different roles in the reading process, multiple parts of the brain are in constant collaboration when tasked with reading. The three major brain regions linked to reading and phonological analysis include the left temporoparietal region, the left occipitotemporal region, and the inferior frontal gyrus. The temporoparietal and inferior frontal gyrus assist in phonological processing, while the occipitotemporal region helps recognize words by sight. The functions of these regions as they relate to language and reading are summarized in the table below.

Brain Region	Location	Function
Left Parieto-Temporal Region	Back	Used to process spoken language and help us understand speech sounds and what words mean. This area is important for mapping letters and written words to their written correspondences. We also use this area for decoding unfamiliar words.
Left Occipital-Temporal Region	Back	Part of the visual processing center at the base of the brain. We use this area to recognize objects and faces, but as we become fluent readers, we use this area for letter recognition, automaticity, and language comprehension.
Inferior Frontal Gyrus	Front	Broca's area in this cortex helps form speech sounds. This area helps readers slowly analyze a word and sound it out, the last step in reading.

Reading Activity in the Brain

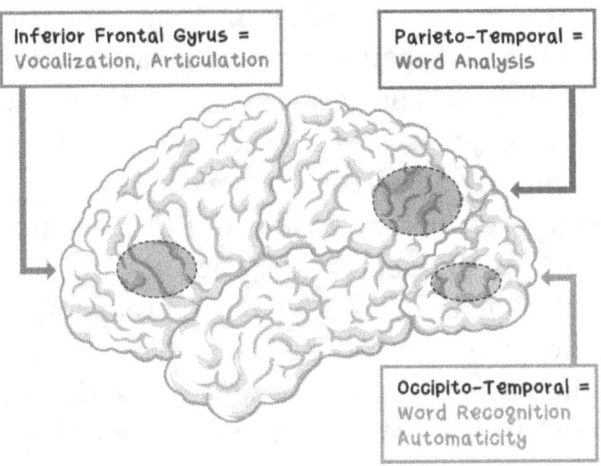

Inferior Frontal Gyrus =
Vocalization, Articulation

Parieto-Temporal =
Word Analysis

Occipito-Temporal =
Word Recognition
Automaticity

As an individual learns to read, the brain will create new circuits that connect the language processing parts of the brain with the visual processing parts. A child's brain will literally change the way it functions as they learn to read. Brain imaging research by Cunningham and Rose has revealed that activation patterns in areas of the brain will be different depending on an individual's reading ability. For example, beginning readers show more activity in the temporoparietal region as they decode, while more experienced readers become increasingly active in the occipitotemporal region as they can recognize more words automatically by sight.

A Dyslexic Brain

Brain imaging of struggling readers shows that patterns of activity are notably different compared to proficient readers. The neural pathways for language and cognition are not as efficient and established, which causes weak phonological processing. According to the American Speech-Language-Hearing Association (ASHA), phonological processing is the "use of the sounds of one's language (i.e., phonemes) to process spoken and written language." When a child is unable to process speech sounds accurately, the brain's neurons have more difficulty connecting to form the collaborative network needed to map sounds to letters for skilled reading and spelling.

When reading, a dyslexic individual shows under-activation in areas in the back of the brain (temporoparietal region and occipitotemporal region) and over-activation in other areas to compensate. They rely more on their frontal lobe, which is why they sound out each word and have difficulty recognizing words by sight. Additionally, instead of using areas of the brain in the left hemisphere, which is designed to process language, struggling readers often use different parts of the right hemisphere, which is not efficient. Furthermore, neuroscientists have found that struggling readers tend to have less gray and white matter in the left parietal area. Reduced gray matter may adversely affect their ability to accurately process the different sounds of language, while decreased white matter may impact the overall reading processing efficiency of the brain.

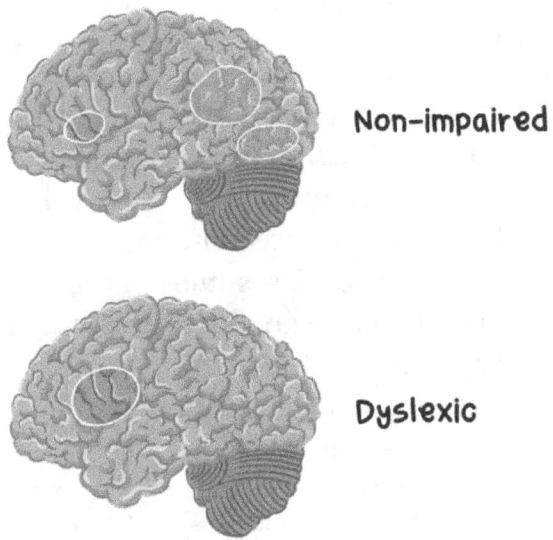

The visual above illustrates how the dyslexic brain is activated more in the frontal region, while the non-dyslexic brain is activated in several parts of the left hemisphere.

Not All Phonics Instruction Creates Equal Brain Activation

As explained in this chapter, the brain must rewire and form neural connections between the language and visual processing centers of the brain to read. However, the brain responds differently to different literacy approaches. The chart below summarizes the three most popular reading approaches—Whole Language, Balanced Literacy, and Structured Literacy—and how the brain is activated when individuals utilize each approach.

Literacy Approach	Description	Brain Activation
Whole Language	This approach believes that phonics instruction is boring and doesn't build a love of reading. This approach assumes that children are born to read and that they will learn to read by being immersed in books.	Activates the right hemisphere, which is consistent with struggling readers.
Balanced Literacy	This approach uses a mix of phonics and the Whole Language approach. However, when phonics is taught, it is not in a direct way and often uses "3-cueing," which encourages children to guess unknown words based on pictures and context. Additionally, children are taught to memorize high-frequency words.	Reading words through memorization activates the right hemisphere, which is consistent with struggling readers.
Structured Literacy	An explicit, systematic, and diagnostic way to	Activation in the left hemisphere

	teach reading. This approach teaches the structure of language through phonology, sound-symbol correspondences, syllables, morphology, syntax, and semantics. This approach builds foundational skills in a way that helps all students but is especially beneficial for struggling readers. Children are taught the "reading code" and are encouraged to sound out unknown words.	of the brain, especially in the language and visual processing centers, which is a hallmark of skilled readers.

While some children's brains can rewire and learn to read using the Whole Language or Balanced Literacy approach, these approaches are not the most optimal, especially for those who are at-risk or are already struggling.

Rewiring the Dyslexic Brain

The brain is extremely malleable, which is why it has the capacity to rewire itself for reading. Although all learners need to build these pathways, individuals with dyslexia have atypical brain development and will *only* develop these pathways using an approach to reading that coincides with how the brain needs to rewire.

More specifically, they need an approach that uses explicit, structured phonics instruction called Structured Literacy that is scientifically proven to connect and activate the language processing and visual processing centers of the brain in the left hemisphere. Additionally, they must participate in phonemic awareness activities that will strengthen their weakened phonological processing skills. This instruction helps the brain perceive individual sounds and sound sequences in words, which is necessary for learning the alphabetic code.

Although dyslexia is a life-long disability, by learning to read using this approach, they will learn to read text automatically, fluently, and with comprehension. Various studies have been conducted that illustrate the changing brain functions as a dyslexic child receives remediation using a Structured Literacy approach. See below for a set of fMRI images.

Evidence From Functional fMRI

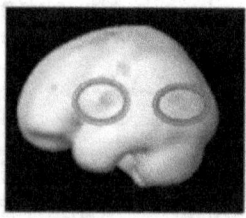 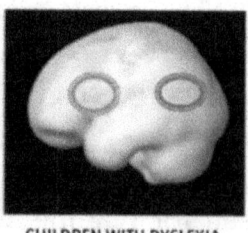 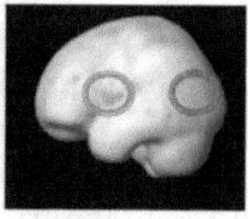

TYPICALLY READING CHILDREN   CHILDREN WITH DYSLEXIA
                               BEFORE REMEDIATION

CHILDREN WITH DYSLEXIA
AFTER REMEDIATION

*Image from presentation by Dr. Nadine Gaab, Reading and the Brain

Summary

Our brains aren't hardwired to read. Instead, brain regions that serve other functions such as spoken language and object recognition are reorganized and connected when a child learns the letters and their sounds and begins to decode written language. Unfortunately, not all brains form these neural connections efficiently, which ultimately slows down the reading process. Although dyslexia is a lifelong disability, individuals can learn to read when provided with evidence-based literacy instruction that will ultimately rewire their brains for reading.

Biography

Brittany Zucker, M.S. CCC-SLP, TSSLD, C-SLDI, A/OGA, is a language and literacy interventionist based in New York City who specializes in treating children with reading and spelling weaknesses, receptive and expressive language disorders, and language-based learning disabilities, including dyslexia. She works full-time at a private school for students with dyslexia where she mentors and coaches reading teachers and provides evidence-based language intervention and structured, multisensory literacy instruction. After school, she sees clients privately and works collaboratively with parents to ensure their children are receiving the best and most appropriate support in the classroom. Brittany strives to have a meaningful impact on the rate of learning improvement for those who are diagnosed with or are at-risk for language-based reading difficulties.

Brittany is ASHA (American Speech-Language-Hearing Association) certified, holds a teacher of students with speech and language disabilities (TSSLD) certification, is a dyslexia interventionist through the International Dyslexia Association (IDA), and is certified at the associate level through the Academy of Orton Gillingham (OGA). You can find Brittany on Instagram @bzlanguageandliteracy and through her website www.bzlanguageandliteracy.com.

References

Cunningham, A. & Rose, D. *This is your brain on reading.* Retrieved from https://www.hmhco.com/products/iread/pdfs/EdWeek_OpEd5_brain_on_reading.pdf

Dehaene, S. (2009). *Reading in the brain.* New York, Penguin Group.

Eden, G.F. *Dyslexia and the brain.* International Dyslexia Society. Retrieved from https://app.box.com/s/q2cjihwikwncohy3vmv747h04md6eevn

Eden, G.F. (2016). *Dyslexia and the brain.* YouTube video. Posted by Understood, Oct 14, 2016. Retrieved from https://www.youtube.com/watch?v=QrF6m1mRsCQ

Hudson, N., Scheff, J., Tarsha, M., & Cutting, L.E. (2016). Reading comprehension and executive function: Neurobiological findings. *Perspectives on Language and Literacy,* Spring 2016.

Huber, E., Donnelly, P.M., Rokem, A. (2018). Rapid and widespread white matter plasticity during an intensive reading intervention. *Nat Commun.,* 9, 2260. Retrieved from https://doi.org/10.1038/s41467-018-04627-5

Hudson, R.F., High, L., & Al Otaiba, S. (2007). Dyslexia and the brain: What does current research tell us? *The Reading Teacher,* 60(6), 506-515.

Seidenberg, M. (2018). *Language at the speed of sight.* New York: Basic Books.

Shaywitz, S. (2003). *Overcoming Dyslexia.* New York: Alfred A. Knopf.

Shaywitz, B.A., Shaywitz, S.E., Pugh, K.R., Mencl, W.E., Fulbright, R.K., Skudlarksi, P., et al. (2002). Disruption of posterior brain systems for reading in children with developmental dyslexia. *Biological Psychiatry,* 52, 101-110.

Chapter 3
Dyslexia State Legislation

By Lauren McClenney-Rosenstein, Ed.D., A/OGA

"Once you learn to read, you will be forever free."

- Frederick Douglass

Starting my career in 2011 at a private dyslexic school in the suburbs of Georgia, I didn't know anything about dyslexia until I was Orton-Gillingham (OG) trained by an Orton-Gillingham fellow. Because I was in a specialized private school with excellent resources (OG fellow on campus, teachers who were already trained and certified, etc.), I didn't *need* to understand the dyslexia laws in the public school system, but I was very active in the International Dyslexia Association (IDA) Georgia branch as an aspiring OG practitioner. When I was employed in the state of Georgia, there weren't any laws, just organizations that supported the dyslexia cause such as IDA GA and Decoding Dyslexia GA (DDGA). Georgia did not create a law until 2019, which focuses on screening and services.

After leaving Georgia, I taught in another specialized private school in Washington, D.C. where I taught struggling readers using the Orton-Gillingham methodology. Again, because I was in a specialized private school, understanding the dyslexia laws in the DC public school system was not the main focus. But having interviewed a special education lawyer in 2020, who is barred and practices in the District of Columbia, it became abundantly clear that Washington, D.C., our nation's capital, didn't get it together until 2020 when they passed a law for Dyslexia Screening and Prevention Pilot Programs.

It wasn't until I began teaching in a public school in the state of Maryland that I realized I needed to truly pay attention to what the laws were saying about what could and could not be on an individualized education plan (IEP). I remember being a part of Decoding Dyslexia MD, fighting side by side with moms who were pushing to get this law passed for a dyslexia screener, which became a law in 2019. I was on my way out of the public school system at this point. The overall theme I found was that each state functioned differently and while each state had their own Decoding Dyslexia chapter, each state now has their own laws put in place.

North Atlantic Region: MA, NY, PA, NJ, DE, CT, MD, DC, RI, ME, NH, VT

State	Current Dyslexia Laws	State Dyslexia Guides & Handbooks	Past Legislation/ Revisions
MA	Students with Dyslexia (2018)	N/A	Exempting students with dyslexia from standardized college entrance exams (1983) Students with Dyslexia (2018)
NY	Education Guidance Memorandum (2017)	N/A	Education Guidance Memorandum (2017)
PA	Dyslexia Intervention Pilot Program (2014)	N/A	Dyslexia Intervention Pilot Program (2014)

NJ	Screening for Dyslexia (2013)	New Jersey Dyslexia Handbook A Guide to Early Literacy Development & Reading Struggles (September 2017) 53 pages	Screening for Dyslexia (2013) Definitions relative to Reading Disabilities (2013) Professional Development Related to Disabilities (2013)
DE	Alternate forms of assessment for LD students; IEP and intervention for children not reading at age 7 (2015)	N/A	N/A

CT	Dyslexia Law Implementation Task Force (2021)	N/A	Dyslexia Assessment & Instruction; Teacher Training (2017; 2016; 2015) Dyslexia Law Implementation Task Force (2019)

MD	Dyslexia Screening (2019)	Maryland Technical Assistance Bulletin SPECIFIC LEARNING DISABILITY & SUPPLEMENT (Focus on Dyslexia, Dyscalculia, and Dysgraphia). Maryland State Department of Education (November 7, 2016) 14 pages	Dyslexia Screening (2019)
DC	Dyslexia Screening and Prevention Pilot Program (2020)	N/A	N/A

RI	Education of Children with Dyslexia (2019)	N/A	Dyslexia-targeted literacy assistance (2016) Right To Read Act (2019)
ME	Dyslexia Screening; Dyslexia Coordinator (2015)	N/A	Dyslexia Screening; Dyslexia Coordinator (2015)
NH	Screening and Intervention for Dyslexia (2016)	New Hampshire Resource Guide A Resource Guide for Dyslexia and Other Related Disorders. New Hampshire Department of Education. 57 pages	Screening and Intervention for Dyslexia (2016)
VT	N/A	N/A	N/A

South Atlantic Region: VA, NC, SC, GA, FL

State	Current Dyslexia Law	State Dyslexia Guides & Handbooks	Past Legislation/ Revisions
VA	Reading Standards & Intervention (2021) Special Education Policies & Procedures (2021)	N/A	Dyslexia Advisor in Public Schools (2017) Teacher Training, Dyslexia Awareness (2016) Required university coursework in dyslexia (2018)
NC	Students with Dyslexia and Dyscalculia (2017)	North Carolina Dyslexia Topic Brief Public Schools of North Carolina, Exceptional Children Division (2019) 17 pages	Students with Dyslexia and Dyscalculia (2017)

SC	Universal Screening (2018)	South Carolina Dyslexia Handbook South Carolina Department of Education (September 2020) 69 pages	Universal Screening (2018)
GA	Dyslexia Screening & Services (2019)	N/A	N/A
FL	Early Learning & Student Literacy (2021)	N/A	N/A School Community Professional Development Act (2017)

Great Lakes Region: OH, WV, MI

State	Current Dyslexia Law	State Dyslexia Guides & Handbooks	Past Legislation/ Revisions
OH	Pilot Project - Early Intervention and Screening (2012)	N/A	Pilot Project - Early Intervention and Screening (2012)
WV	Dyslexia and dyscalculia defined (2014)	N/A	Dyslexia and dyscalculia defined (2014)
MI	N/A	N/A	N/A

South Eastern Region: TN, AL, MS

State	Current Dyslexia Law	State Dyslexia Guides & Handbooks	Past Legislation/ Revisions
TN	Dyslexia Advisory Board (2020)	Tennessee Dyslexia Resource Guide Tennessee Department of Education (2018) 44 pages	Dyslexia Screening and Intervention (2019; 2016)
			Required Accommodations for Dyslexia on State Licensing Exams (2019)
			Literacy Success Act (2021)
			Dyslexia Advisory Board (2018)

AL	Alabama Literacy Act (2019)	Alabama Dyslexia Resource Guide Alabama State Board of Education (October 27, 2016 revision) 77 pages (archived version)	Dyslexia provisions of Administrative Code (2015)
MS	Dyslexia Education Requirements (2021)	Mississippi Best Practices Dyslexia Handbook Mississippi Department of Education, Office of Curriculum and Instruction (2010) 44 pages	Dyslexia Therapy Scholarship (2017, 2012) Pilot programs for testing and educational remediation for dyslexia and related disorders. (2007, 2001, 1999, 1997, 1996, 1994) Loan Forgiveness for Dyslexia Teachers (2019)

South Central Region: AR, LA, NM, TX

State	Current Dyslexia Law	State Dyslexia Guides & Handbooks	Past Legislation/ Revisions
AR	Certified Academic Language Therapist (2021)	Arkansas Dyslexia Resource Guide Arkansas Department of Education, 2017 (66 pages)	Dyslexia Definition, Screening, Instruction (2017; 2015) Right to Read Act (2019) Required Dyslexia Services for Incarcerated Youth and Adults (2019)

| LA | Early Literacy (2021) | Louisiana Guide to Dyslexia Louisiana Department of Education (July 2021) 6 pages

Louisiana Regulations and Guidelines Bulletin 1903— Regulations and Guidelines for Implementation of the Louisiana Law for the Education of Dyslexic Students (2021) 30 pages | Dyslexia Testing and Remediation (2013)

Decisions of Board of Parole: Exempting individuals with dyslexia from certain conditions premised on educational attainment (2010, 2009)

Testing pupils' sight and hearing; testing for dyslexia; (2005, 2003, 1990, 1989, 1987, 1986)

Duties of State Board of Elementary and Secondary Education (2010 (numerous amendments since 1975) |

LA (cont.)			Screening and Intervention for School Success (2021, 1997, 1992) Revised Definition of Dyslexia (2020)
NM	Intervention for students displaying characteristics of dyslexia. (2010)	N/A	Intervention for students displaying characteristics of dyslexia. (2010)

| TX | Monitoring School Compliance (2021) | Texas Dyslexia Handbook, 2021 Update. Procedures Concerning Dyslexia and Related Disorders. Texas Education Agency (2021) 83 pages | Classroom technology for dyslexia (2011)

Screening and Treatment for Dyslexia and Related Disorders (2019, 2017, 2011, 1995)

Educator Preparation for Dyslexia (2021, 2011)

Licensed Dyslexia Practitioners and Licensed Dyslexia Therapists (2015; 2009)

Retesting University Students for Dyslexia (2011) |

TX (cont.)			Examination Accommodations For Persons With Dyslexia (2011)
			Dyslexia Specialist at Regional Centers (2017)
			Monitoring School Compliance (2019)
			School District Dyslexia Allotment (2019)
			Special Education Transition Planning (2017)

Central Region: WI, IL, IN, KY, MN, ND, SD

State	Current Dyslexia Law	State Dyslexia Guides & Handbooks	Past Legislation/Revisions
WI	Dyslexia Guidebook (2020)	N/A	Dyslexia Guidebook (2020)

| IL | Definition of Dyslexia and Advisory group (2016) | Illinois - The Dyslexia Guide

A Handbook for Parents, Educators, and Students \| ISBE Division of Special Education Services (July 2019) 27 pages

Reading Instruction Best Practices Related to Dyslexia (June 2016) 3 pages | Definition of Dyslexia and Advisory group (2014) |

| IN | Dyslexia Screening and Intervention (2018) | N/A | Dyslexia Definition; Teacher Training (2015)

Dyslexia Screening and Intervention (2018) |
| KY | Ready to Read Act (2018) | N/A | Early Education Assessment and Intervention (2012)

Definitions of Dyslexia and Related Terms (2012) |

MN	Dyslexia Identification & Screening (2019) Teacher Education Programs (2019)	Minnesota - Navigating the School System When a Child is Struggling with Reading or Dyslexia Minnesota Department of Education (April 2015) 47 pages	Reading Proficiency; Dyslexia Reporting (2016) Definition of Dyslexia (2015) Dyslexia Specialist (2017)
ND	Dyslexia Identification & Screening (2019) Teacher Education Programs (2019)	North Dakota Department of Public Instruction, Dyslexia Resources	Reading Proficiency; Dyslexia Reporting (2016) Definition of Dyslexia (2015) Dyslexia Specialist (2017)

SD	Define Dyslexia (2020)	South Dakota The Dyslexia Handbook for Teachers and Parents South Dakota Department of Education (Revised April 2021) 30 pages	Define Dyslexia (2020)

Mid-Western Region: IA, NE, KS, MO, OK, CO, MT, WY

State	Current Dyslexia Law	State Dyslexia Guides & Handbooks	Past Legislation/ Revisions

IA	Dyslexia Definition & Teacher Training (2020)	N/A	Dyslexia Assistance (2014) Teacher Training (2016) Dyslexia Definition & Teacher Training (2020)
NE	Dyslexia Screening and Intervention (2018)	Nebraska Department of Education Dyslexia Guide	Adds and defines dyslexia for purposes of special education (2017)
KS	N/A	Kansas Dyslexia Initiatives Kansas State Department of Education webpage	N/A
MO	Dyslexia Screening (2016)	N/A	Policy for Reading Intervention (2012)

OK	State Dyslexia Handbook (2021)	N/A	Pilot Dyslexia Teacher Training Program (2012)
			Definition of Specific Learning Disability including Dyslexia (2016, 2018)
			Annual Dyslexia Awareness Training in Schools (2019)
			Required Dyslexia Screening (2020)
CO	Pilot Program for Dyslexia (2020)	Colorado Dyslexia Handbook Colorado Departmen t of Education (2020) 90 pages	Assessment and identification of students with literacy challenges including dyslexia (2019) Pilot Program for Dyslexia (2019)

| MT | Montana Dyslexia Screening and Intervention Act (2019) | N/A | Montana Dyslexia Screening and Intervention Act (2019) |
| WY | Assessment and Early Intervention (2019) | N/A | Assessment and Early Intervention (2012) |

Western Region: AK, AZ, CA, HI, ID, NV, OR, UT, WA

State	Current Dyslexia Law	State Dyslexia Guides & Handbooks	Past Legislation/ Revisions
AK	Legislative Task Force on Reading Proficiency and Dyslexia (2018)	N/A	N/A

AZ	Dyslexia Screening & Intervention (2021)	Arizona Dyslexia Handbook Arizona Department of Education (March 2018) 50 pages	Dyslexia Screening & Intervention (2021, 2019, 2018, 2017, 2015) Dyslexia Handbook (2017)

CA	Teacher Credentialing (2021)	California Dyslexia Guidelines California Department of Education (2018) 136 pages	Teacher Training: "Encourages" universities and schools to provide training in recognizing and teaching for dyslexia (2007, 1990) Definitions and Eligibility for Special Education Services (2011, 1992) Special Education: Dyslexia program guidelines (2015)
HI	N/A	N/A	N/A
ID	N/A	N/A	N/A

NV	Dyslexia Screening and Services (2015)	Nevada's Dyslexia Resource Guide Nevada Department of Education (October 2015) 38 pages	Dyslexia Screening and Services (2015)
OR	Dyslexia Provisions (2017)	N/A	Dyslexia Provisions (2015)
UT	Interventions for Reading Difficulties Program (2019)	N/A	Interventions for Reading Difficulties Program (2015)

WA	Individuals with dyslexia — Identification and instruction (2009)	Washington State Dyslexia Resource Guide Prepared by Washington Branch of the International Dyslexia Association (WABIDA) in collaboration with OSPI Reading Office (November 2011) 75 pages	Individuals with dyslexia — Identification and instruction (2009)

In a perfect world, it would be ideal for ALL states to have a comprehensive dyslexia handbook and laws protecting parent and child rights, what's involved in getting diagnosed with dyslexia, and what necessary steps there are for accommodations. In theory, all teacher preparation programs should be training their teachers in the Science of Reading and equipping them with the formula for success to know how to identify, screen, assess, and teach these language-based learners. We know that teacher preparation programs at the college/university level do not teach this, and if they do, the level of depth varies by program, instructor, and curriculum. We are past the age of screeners. While screeners are helpful to gather data, it's not enough.

We need to take the screening to the next level of diagnosis and interventions. It would be ideal to have Orton-Gillingham fellows work regionally with school districts to properly train elementary educators about the methodology and approach to not only get them exposed but also equip them to walk into a class and know exactly what to do to intervene at a young age. I look back at 2011, and I do see progress in how far we've come in the dyslexia world, but there's still so much more that we need to do as a whole to truly move the needle forward.

Biography

Dr. Lauren McClenney-Rosenstein's passion for educating, advocating, and bringing awareness to dyslexia at the domestic and international levels began in the elementary classrooms of private schools serving students with language-based learning disabilities. She has been a certified special educator for a decade, and she earned her doctor of education in teaching, learning, leadership, and curriculum in 2019 from Northeastern University and holds a dual master's in special education and elementary education from Syracuse University and a bachelor's degree in psychology from Syracuse University.

Her dedication to providing the gold standard of instruction to individuals with dyslexia led her to obtain her endorsement at the associate level through The Orton-Gillingham Academy in 2014. Eventually, she expanded her skill set in the public schools as a seventh and eighth grade math and English Language Arts (ELA) co-teacher before taking a position with a nonprofit organization that advocates for inclusion in public schools for students with disabilities. Currently, Dr. Lauren is a middle school learning specialist and instructional coach at a private school in Baltimore, MD, while also the CEO of Think Dyslexia LLC. Follow her on Instagram @thedrlauren.

Chapter 4
SLP Assessment

By Danelle Augustine, M.A., CCC-SLP, CALT

"Assessment is today's means of modifying tomorrow's instruction."

- Carol Ann Tomlinson

Dyslexia has been part of my life in a larger way than just my profession or my career. My husband is a 32-year-old talented, gifted, and dyslexic HVAC technician. His empathy, intuition, social skills, and ability to understand people better than they understand themselves has always astounded me. He never received a diagnosis or intervention as a child. In fact, I assisted with his diagnosis in adulthood after gifting him a book while we were dating and being agitated that he never read it. That's when I learned that his reason for not partaking in my thoughtful girlfriend gift went all the way back to his first-grade classroom. He vividly remembers sitting in class, looking down at a worksheet and having absolutely no idea what to do with it. He remembers looking around at the other kids, and at six years old, he knew that he was not like the other kids in his class. He still has difficulty with sequencing the syllables correctly in multisyllabic words. The word "obnoxious" is always a fun challenge for him to say in our house. Having such a smart and beautiful person grow into adulthood with the belief that they are "stupid" is a tragedy, especially when the information is out there and we know how to assess, treat, and walk with these children and their families through their journey.

As speech-language pathologists, there are many uncertainties and questions as to our role in the assessment of dyslexia. Should we participate in assessing only oral language? Should we have any input on the individual's phonological awareness skills? Do we let the neuropsychologist or educational diagnostician just do what they need to do and send the kid to us if they need language or articulation therapy?

These are all questions that I asked myself when I was doing my clinical fellowship year at a public school in Houston, TX. But before we ask the who and the how, we need to make sure that we understand the why.

The International Dyslexia Association (IDA) highlights differences in the terms "testing" versus "evaluation." Considering our profession, I don't feel the need to highlight the importance of the words that we use, especially when you are communicating with and educating parents. IDA states the following:

"When a child is struggling to read, someone will probably suggest that he or she be tested for dyslexia. What does it mean to be tested? You might think of a test as something you take in an afternoon. Someone scores it and tells you how you did. 'Evaluation' is a more accurate word to describe the process of determining if someone has dyslexia. The word 'evaluation' encompasses identification, screening, testing, diagnosis, and all the other information gathering involved when the student, his or her family, and a team of professionals work together to determine why the student is having difficulty and what can be done to help."

Assessment is not only informative, but it is also powerful for individuals and families to understand why they or their child is having difficulties. Assessment and identification have the power to erase the words "dumb" or "stupid" from a child's self-talk and self-image.

As we dive into assessment, let's first look at the definition of "dyslexia" from IDA. The IDA defines *Dyslexia as:*

> a specific learning disability that is neurobiological in origin. It is characterized by difficulties with accurate and/or fluent word recognition and by poor spelling and decoding abilities. These difficulties typically result from a deficit in the phonological component of language that is often unexpected in relation to other cognitive abilities and the provision of effective classroom instruction. Secondary consequences may include problems in reading comprehension and reduced reading experience that can impede growth of vocabulary and background knowledge (Lyon et al., 2003).

I encourage you to refer to this definition as we discuss the specific skills that should be included within a dyslexia assessment, as well as when thinking of your role as a speech-language pathologist.

Similarly, dyslexia screeners are a useful tool for written language disorders, but they will not substitute for a full formal evaluation. Screeners are excellent for school-wide administration to identify those who are "at-risk," but as we know, a full comprehensive evaluation is more helpful.

Skills you will see commonly assessed in evidence-based dyslexia screeners in the earlier years (pre-K-first grade) include phonological awareness, rapid naming, and memory. If you're thinking, "Wow, this sounds like many of the kids I see for speech therapy at that age," your intuition is spot-on. A history of speech, language, and phonological awareness difficulties are a significant risk factor for the diagnosis of dyslexia. Once a child is toward the end of first or second grade, you will see screeners begin to focus more on word decoding and spelling.

Your knowledge about screeners vs. formal assessments in the speech and language realm also applies here. Screeners are brief, and purely utilized to identify at-risk students. A formal evaluation is used to diagnose and for treatment planning.

Here are common evidenced-based screeners you may see:

- Predictive Assessment of Reading (PAR)

- Dynamic Indicators of Basic Early Literacy Skills (DIBELS)
- Texas Primary Reading Inventory (TPRI)
- AIMSweb screening assessments
- Shaywitz Dyslexia Screener

What is in a Dyslexia Assessment?

Background Information

Just like a speech and language evaluation, background information is a must for dyslexia evaluations. Collecting information from parents and teachers about the child's overall skills, strengths, and weaknesses provides a more complete picture than results from a single test or assessment battery. We need to understand their academic history, grades, and attendance. We must rule out school attendance as part of why the student may be struggling. If the student has significant school absences, that could possibly be part of why the student is struggling.

We must also know if there is a history of previous intervention, including speech therapy (since we now know that the history of speech difficulties is a risk factor for dyslexia). I find the history of intervention to be extremely important when you begin looking at the type of intervention the child received and how long they received it, and the most important question is, "Did it work?" Although this chapter is not about intervention, understanding the different types of interventions children may have received is important for the assessment. Dyslexia intervention will be discussed in a later chapter.

Family History

You're probably wondering why family history would not be included in background information. This is because family history deserves its own section. But why? According to Shaywitz, "Children with a history of dyslexia within their immediate family have a substantial risk of being dyslexic" (2003, p.127). When looking at family history I don't just ask, "Does anyone else in your family have a dyslexia diagnosis?" Unfortunately, because so many have gone undiagnosed, you may have to dig a little bit deeper for the answer to this question. Here's a list of other questions you may ask:

- Does anyone in your family have a history of difficulties with school?
- Has anyone in your family had trouble learning to read?
- Does anyone in your family really dislike school?
- Has anyone in your family dropped out of school? If so, why?

When asking about family history we must remember all of the different ways that dyslexia, especially undiagnosed dyslexia, can show up in a person's life.

Oral Language Skills

I'm hoping your SLP eyes brightened up when you saw this section. As SLPs, this is our bread and butter.

Here's a quick refresher for you on the five areas of language:

1. Phonology
2. Morphology
3. Semantics
4. Syntax
5. Pragmatics

Now let's talk about these areas of language within the context of dyslexia.

Although no two children with dyslexia are exactly alike, there are some themes that you will notice when you assess their language skills. According to Shaywitz, et.al, "The core deficit for dyslexics is phonological processing," (1996). We will discuss this in the following section.

Children with dyslexia may have oral language difficulties that go beyond phonological processing, but these do not always occur. It is important to know that a child can be diagnosed with specific language impairment (SLI) and dyslexia if there are other significant oral language difficulties with semantics, syntax, etc. (Catts, Adlof, Hogan, & Weismer, 2005)

Phonological Processing

Phonological processing is known as the *core deficit* for children with dyslexia.

You'll see weaknesses in the following subsets of phonological processing:

- Phonological awareness: Awareness of sounds in language **enter awesome SLP skills here**
- Phonological memory: Memory for the speech sounds in words, i.e., letter names, names of numbers
- Phonological retrieval: Word and name retrieval
- Phonological production: The ability to produce more phonologically complex or multisyllabic words, i.e., how my husband has difficulty sequencing the syllables and saying the word "obnoxious"

Vocabulary knowledge

As SLPs we teach vocabulary, or semantics, every day. Children with dyslexia may present with deficits in oral language as well as deficits in memory. As children progress into third, fourth, and fifth grades, we know that independent reading is associated with vocabulary development. When children with dyslexia are not identified and provided with intervention, reading is *hard*. If reading is hard, stressful, and anxiety-provoking, they aren't going to do it. We then see an ever-widening gap between them and their non-dyslexic peers in the area of vocabulary. Although the deficits begin with poor phonological processing skills, over time it evolves into lack of exposure.

Word Recognition

This section and the following sections are where we get into what may feel more foreign to you as a speech-language pathologist. This is where we get into the actual reading of words.

Word recognition is looking at the ability to read *single* words. Students with dyslexia are not able to use clues from the sentence or background knowledge about the topic to know what the word says. In my experience, children with dyslexia who have adequate oral language skills outside of phonological processing use those language skills to aid in their guessing of words when reading aloud. On the other hand, single word recognition takes the language aspect out of it.

For example, a child may be able to read the word "flower" in a sentence like, "She was walking in the meadow and looked down to pick the tall, beautiful yellow flower." Yet they are unable to recognize "flower" on its own. There are semantic clues in the sentence, and likely in the sentences before this, to help a child use their higher-level oral language skills to recognize the word "flower."

Decoding

I've seen SLPs sometimes confuse "decoding" with "word recognition," so let's talk about the differences here. As stated earlier, *word recognition* is the ability to read the actual words, even outside the context of language, aka: in a sentence or paragraph. *Decoding* is about letter sound knowledge, their ability to match the letter or a group of letters with their appropriate sound, and blending them together to form a word. Many decoding assessments utilize a tool called "nonsense words." These words are not real words, but you can apply the same phonological rules of our language to be able to read them.

Here are some examples:

- Tup
- Fost
- Starbing
- Mistudge
- Vopiphonia

Spelling

Spelling is one of the most difficult skills for those with dyslexia. The process of spelling is the opposite process of word recognition. For word recognition, the child must look at the letters and letter sequences and blend them together to create one word.

For spelling, the child must take the sounds apart in a given word and assign their correct letters or letter sequences to each sound.

Here is a higher-level example:

Judge has three sounds or phonemes, but it has 5 letters.

JUDGE

/dʒ/ /ʌ/ /dʒ/

Spelling is difficult because it is taxing on long- and short-term memory. We must also integrate motor skills to physically write the letters. You can imagine, if there is a deficit in any one of these areas, the weekly spelling list can be a source of anxiety.

Rapid Automatic Naming

You may also hear this referred to as "automaticity" or "fluency skills." Children with dyslexia typically have slower processing speeds for information (both visual and auditory). Also keep in mind, rapid automatic naming is related to the phonological processing deficit of processing auditory information. Tasks to assess the skill may look like rows of colors, numbers, or objects, and the child must name each one as quickly as they can. This skill is also often used in an earlier diagnosis of dyslexia (before second grade).

Reading Comprehension

It is important to note that when assessing reading comprehension, we must keep in mind that children with dyslexia may perform poorly on reading comprehension assessments due to their difficulty with decoding. Some dyslexic students may also perform within the average range if they are able to rely on higher-level language skills to help them understand the whole meaning of the passage. Therefore, an average reading comprehension score does not necessarily mean the child is not dyslexic. In my experience, I like to look at reading comprehension scores and listening comprehension scores to see if there is a significant disparity.

Reading Fluency

Reading fluency has been defined as the ability to read with appropriate speed, accuracy, and expression. As SLPs, we may refer to "expression" as "appropriate intonation." When a child has trouble with reading fluency, it's difficult to listen to them struggle through a sentence or a paragraph. When they are faced with a long passage to read, you will see their eyes widen and fatigue set in as they read. Deficits in reading fluency are really the culmination of all of the smaller deficits that you will see with dyslexia. The poor phonological processing, the poor word recognition, the poor decoding will all show up in the child's ability to read an age-appropriate text fluently.

Assessing this skill typically requires the reader to read a grade- or age-level passage while the assessor documents the number of words read correctly and the number of errors. This will give you a WCPM (words correct per minute). Common reading fluency assessments are DIBELS (Dynamic Indicators of Basic Literacy Skills) and the GORT-5 (Gray Oral Reading Test, fifth edition).

Intelligence Testing

There is still a commonly held belief that in order to assess and diagnose dyslexia, you must have some form of intelligence testing. According to Shaywitz, "the discovery of the phonologic model has drastically diminished the role of tests of intelligence in the diagnosis of Dyslexia" (2003).

Traditionally, the concept of dyslexia as an "unexpected" difficulty in reading was interpreted as an underachievement and reading relative to ability (or learning potential). In other words, simply knowing a person's IQ should have predicted his level of reading achievement," (p. 136). She later goes on to explain how those procedures were established before we truly understood the role of phonology and phonological processing in reading difficulties.

Simply put, we used to think that you had to have poor reading achievement paired with average to above average intelligence in order to be diagnosed with dyslexia. Thanks to our better understanding of how reading actually works in the brain, IQ is not a determining factor in diagnosing dyslexia, and you do not have to perform an IQ test to diagnose.

We must also remember the cycle in which dyslexia limits the child's reading abilities and their desire to read, therefore impacting their vocabulary development. Due to these reasons, IQ scores can be artificially lowered.

I find that, as speech-language pathologists, we have an easier time understanding this distinction. We understand that language skills or difficulties with language do not equate to lower intelligence.

I'll put it to you this way: a fourth grader may have difficulty blending c-a-t to make the word "cat" but be able to build his own robot with minimal instructions.

Preponderance of Data

If you are in or have ever worked in the school setting as an SLP, you are probably familiar with your particular district's standards for qualifying for services. Many students qualify if they present with scores 1.5 standard deviations below the mean. Districts may have very similar standards for qualifying for Specific Learning Disability—dyslexia. For example, in the state of Louisiana, there are standards where the child must show a pattern of strengths and weaknesses. A strength would be quantified as no more than .5 standard deviations below the mean in grades 1 and 2, etc.

Preponderance of data is important for both private and school assessments because it allows the assessor to examine other measures besides standard scores. We know in our profession that a standard score does not always paint a clear picture of what is going on with a child. Therefore, a trained and qualified assessor can use a preponderance of data to support their decision that a student has dyslexia.

The following quote is from Louisiana Bulletin 1508, a regulatory guide for the state of Louisiana on the evaluation of students who are possibly in need of special education services:

La. Admin. Code tit. 28 § CI-719

When the combination of the scientifically research-based intervention outcomes and standardized testing does not result in clearly established strengths

71

and weaknesses, but a preponderance of all data collected supports the team's position that the student is a student with a specific learning disability, a full explanation and justification must be included in the evaluation report.

Differences in Setting

One frustrating issue I've seen throughout my career and part of the reason why this book is in your hands is confusion with the definition of dyslexia, the diagnosis of dyslexia, and what "qualifies" a child for dyslexia or reading services in the schools or any other kind of setting.

Similarly, with speech therapy services, there is a difference between "qualifying for services" in a private setting versus in a school setting. The purpose of an evaluation through the school system is to determine if there is an "educational impact," whereas the purpose of a private evaluation does not necessarily rely on school performance.

Typically, schools like to perform their own evaluations, and function on their own diagnostic criteria. This can vary from state to state or even district to district. For example, in my state of Louisiana, we utilize Bulletin 1508 as our guideline for special education services. Being diagnosed with dyslexia through a neuropsychologist private practice is not the same as being diagnosed with Specific Learning Disability through a school-based evaluation and qualifying for services through the school system.

It's also important to address the "culture" of who does the reading intervention in a school versus a private setting. Some schools have reading specialists, dyslexia interventionists, or resource teachers. I'm sure you've heard these terms floating around your schools before. There is no central guideline or database for which professional is supposed to do what. This decision is related to the culture of the school, the language used by the district, available resources, and the requirements for special education instructors in a given district or state.

Although the role of speech-language pathologists in dyslexia intervention is crucial, it is often not in the cultural expectations of the school that the SLP will work on reading. I've heard many SLPs say, "Oh, I don't do reading; the reading specialist does that." You can see this cultural expectation more clearly when an SLP pursues continuing education only to be cautioned about "encroaching on someone else's territory." All of these nuances (that every school, district, and state have) can influence how services are delivered and who is delivering them, while having little to do with the actual scope of practice of a speech-language pathologist.

Who can Diagnose Dyslexia?

This is a question that can breed a lot of confusion within the topic of dyslexia. Unfortunately, there is currently no federal law or policy that makes a distinction as to who can diagnose dyslexia and who cannot. Through my own research and practice, I've found it is more about the knowledge and background of the individual or individuals performing the assessment as opposed to someone needing to have a particular set of credentials.

Shaywitz says "...it is administered on an individual basis by a professional who is knowledgeable about reading and dyslexia: a speech and language pathologist, a learning disabilities specialist or an experienced psychologist" (2003, p.143). Notice the initial mention that the professional must be "knowledgeable about reading and dyslexia."

The International Dyslexia Association recommends the following:

> Assessment of dyslexia involves individual testing, most often provided by a team of qualified professionals who have had extensive clinical training in assessment as part of a graduate degree program. Professional clinicians who assess Specific Learning Disabilities (SLD) and dyslexia may have M.A., M.S., M.ED., Ed.D., or Ph.D. degrees in Education, Reading, Speech Language Pathology, School Psychology, Psychology, or Neuropsychology. Evaluation by a medical doctor is not required for assessment or identification of SLD or dyslexia.

As you can see from the examples above, although there are examples of professions that can diagnose, there isn't a clear consensus of who can and cannot diagnose. The individual must have a thorough working knowledge of how students learn to read and how dyslexia may present amongst those skills, as well as an understanding of relevant background information, etc. It also states that a diagnosis can be from an individual or by a team of professionals.

This vague distinction between who can and cannot diagnose has led to debate among fields. Just as there is a culture around dyslexia intervention, there is a culture around dyslexia diagnosis. There are differences in what you will see at a school vs in a private clinic. There can even be variation between school districts. In the same way that reading intervention is typically administered by reading specialists at a school, assessments are often performed by the following professionals: clinical psychologist, neuropsychologist, educational psychologist, or educational diagnostician.

According to the College Board, the body that administers and regulates the SAT/ACT assessments, in order for a student to receive accommodations, the assessment should be performed by a psychologist.

A school district may or may not accept an assessment performed by an SLP for the student to obtain an IEP or 504 accommodations—you may need to work your advocacy muscles here. There have been SLPs who have had their assessments accepted by a college to provide accommodations in that setting.

SLPs and Dyslexia Assessment

As an SLP, you have an appropriate foundation that can be built upon to meet the needs for dyslexia assessment and diagnosis. You may even find yourself on a team of professionals diagnosing dyslexia as the team member providing the oral language assessment for example.

As stated in the previous section, there is no one entity deciding who can and cannot diagnose dyslexia. You as a practitioner must consider your own training, background, and comfort level, as well as the needs and goals of the individuals seeking assessment.

According to Shaywitz, she often looks to speech-language pathologists when assessing younger children because the focus of the evaluation is their spoken language and phonological awareness skills (2003).

When looking towards who is conducting the assessment, it is important to understand the purpose of the assessment, your own training and skills, and the goals of the family/individual. Does the family desire private services from you? Does the family want accommodations for the upcoming ACT or SAT? Are they hoping to be provided with accommodations and an individualized education plan from their school? Does this child need to be evaluated for comorbidities such as ADHD? Are those comorbidities within your scope of practice?

All of these considerations should be taken into account when deciding on who is the most appropriate individual or group to diagnose.

Biography

Danelle Augustine, M.A., CCC-SLP, CALT is a speech-language pathologist and certified academic language therapist (CALT). She has worked with the dyslexic population in a variety of settings: public schools, charter schools, and private practice. In recognizing the need for specialized dyslexia intervention, she obtained her CALT in 2020. She currently owns her own private practice in the Baton Rouge, LA area and works with children ages pre-k through high school for dyslexia intervention. You may find her on Facebook and Instagram @speechgoods.

References

International Dyslexia Association. *Dyslexia assessment: What is it and how can it help?* (2020, March 10). Retrieved from https://dyslexiaida.org/dyslexia-assessment-what-is-it-and-how-can-it-help/.

Lyon, G.R., Shaywitz, S.E., & Shaywitz, B.A. (2003). A definition of dyslexia. *Annals of Dyslexia, 53,* 1–14.

Shaywitz, S. E., & Shaywitz, J. (2003). *Overcoming dyslexia*. First Vintage Books.

Chapter 5
SLP Literacy-Based Interventions

By Christina L. Pompeo, M.S., CCC-SLP

"SLPs don't know more or better. We know different."

- A dear colleague from whom I've learned so much!

I am an SLP in the public schools, and I felt like I was just "going through the motions" for a long time. Then, I began teaching at the graduate level and supervising students in their clinical placements. My work supervising and teaching graduate students reignited my passion for the profession, making me a better clinician.

I figured if I am going to "talk the talk" I needed to "walk the walk." I began connecting the role of cultural and linguistic practices to diversity in home language and literacy experiences, language and literacy development and engagement, and culturally relevant assessment and intervention in school-age children with whom I work. I provide intervention for multiple populations with varying disabilities, have expertise in managing challenging behaviors, ensure every student is included with their general education peers, and apply evidence-based practices. My core values focus on the belief that the power in our field lies in the connection and collaboration we create with others. I have an ability and love for integrating practical, individual experiences and identifying techniques to benefit those I serve—the students, the families, my colleagues, and the community. Always having an eye on how to keep things fresh and exciting, I engage my students, meet them where they are, and empower them to grow and flourish. My love for learning fuels all that I do, and that is how I came to write this chapter.

Speech-language pathologists possess distinct and extensive content knowledge that differs from that of teachers. The American Speech-Language-Hearing Association's position statement on reading and writing asserts that SLPs, "play a critical and direct role in the development of literacy in children and adolescents with communication disorders, including those with severe and multiple disabilities" (ASHA, 2001). While the teacher is trained in instruction, the SLP is trained in intervention.

As a diagnostician and a clinical problem-solver, the SLP has experience in typical and atypical language development and problems, data collection and analysis, the understanding of cognitive-linguistic demands, and recognizing the logic in errors. In relation to phonological awareness, Boudreau & Larson discuss the importance of the SLPs' role on educational teams (2004). The SLPs' knowledge base includes the developmental sequence of phoneme acquisition, the complexity of phoneme production, the categorization and structure of speech sounds within and across words, and the relationship of phonological awareness to other areas of phonological processing. Additionally, SLPs appreciate the complexity of mapping speech-to-print (Boudreau & Larson, 2004). Wasowicz states:

> Very simply defined, speech-to-print refers to the process of mapping from phoneme to grapheme to spell (encode) the spoken word in written form. This is sometimes referred to as phonological encoding. A speech-to-print approach starts with a focus on the spoken word and moves from that starting point to the written word. (2021)

Schuele & Boudreau add:

> SLPs are educated to consider the many factors that influence the successes and failures of individual children: assessing individual performance to identify individual child needs, linking individual assessment to instruction and intervention efforts, engaging children in dynamic assessment or diagnostic teaching to identify effective teaching strategies, scaffolding child success, and differentiating instruction across children. (2008)

Delayed or impaired development of the phonological system (i.e., phonological awareness, memory, and naming) contributes to deficits in the accuracy and speed of word recognition, decoding, and spelling. In addition to phonological awareness and fluency, other language domains such as morphology, syntax, semantics, and comprehension may also be affected (Scarborough, 2005). The SLP's roles and responsibilities with respect to reading and writing include the provision of intervention, as well as the documentation of outcomes (ASHA, 2001). Other roles include consultation and collaboration with teachers, parents, and students, while advocating for effective literacy practices (ASHA, 2001).

Language-Based Interventions

Intervention for dyslexia should include a multisensory structured language approach focusing on decoding, fluency training, vocabulary, and comprehension (American Academy of Pediatrics, 2011). Furthermore, the National Reading Panel (NRP) concluded there are five essential components to teaching reading. "The Big Five" includes phonemic awareness, the alphabetic principle (i.e., phonics), fluency, vocabulary, and comprehension (NRP, 2000). For the purposes of this chapter, intervention will focus on five areas: phonemic awareness (with instruction on how the alphabet works), fluency, morphology, semantics, and comprehension. Additionally, individuals with dyslexia typically experience difficulty with spelling because reading and spelling are related abilities. Errors in spelling tend to mirror errors in reading. Spelling challenges co-occur with decoding challenges, and they are further impacted by working memory and executive function skills (Hebert et al., 2018). These, in turn, affect written expression. Therefore, spelling and writing will be addressed briefly.

Phonemic Awareness

Phonological awareness is a metalinguistic skill in which an individual is demonstrating awareness of the sound structure of words in their language. At the shallow level, this awareness involves tasks such as identifying the number of syllables in words, identifying and generating rhymes, and matching words that begin and end with a particular sound. A deeper, more complex level, phonemic awareness, is correlated with early reading success. Tasks such as isolating, blending, segmenting, and manipulating phonemes are all part of phonemic awareness, and the latter three will be the focus of this section. However, while phonemic awareness is necessary for early word decoding, it is an insufficient foundation for proficient decoding. Once phonemic awareness is established, orthographic knowledge, or letter sound representations, should be introduced (Schuele & Boudreau, 2008).

- Blending Sounds into Words Sequence:
  - Start with continuant sounds and consonant, vowel (CV) and VC word structures (e.g., no, on, so, as, low, all)
  - Next, move to CV and VC word structures with stop sounds (e.g., to, at, do, odd, go, egg)
  - Then CVC words with continuants (e.g., moon, fish)
  - Then CVC words with stops (and continuants) (e.g., cat, fat, dish)
  - Then CCVC words
  - Then CVCC words

- o Finally, words with continuants and stops in various word shapes
- Blending Sounds into Words Sample Activities:
  - o Guess My Word using objects or pictures
  - o Going on a Word Hunt
  - o What's in the Bag?
  - o If You Think You Know the Word, Shout it Out!
  - o Robot Talk
  - o Blending Slide
- Segmenting Sounds Sequence
  - o See Blending Sounds into Words Sequence
  - o These tasks can be done separately or as reciprocal tasks in this sequence
- Segmenting Sounds Sample Activities
  - o Sound Boxes
  - o Segmenting Cheer
  - o Pound and Sound
- Manipulating Sounds in Words Sequence
  - o Start with deleting parts of words (e.g., Say hotdog. Now say hotdog without hot.)
  - o Delete initial sounds
  - o Delete final sounds
  - o Substitute or add initial and final sounds
- Manipulating Sounds in Words Sample Activities
  - o What's Missing?
  - o What's Left?
  - o Stand Up When You Hear Your Silly Sound Name
- Read-Aloud Books for All Phonemic Awareness Skills

        o See Yopp (1995) for an annotated bibliography of read-aloud books for developing phonemic awareness skills

Fluency

Fluency is the ability to read text quickly, accurately, and with expression, and it is thought to be the bridge between word recognition and comprehension (Vaughn & Linan-Thompson, 2004). Reading fluency frees the child to focus on comprehension of the text versus word decoding.

Fluency Sample Activities

- o Teaching Sight Words
- o Modeling and Repeated Reading
- o Repeated Reading with Corrective Feedback
- o Partner Reading
- o Readers' Theater
- o Tape-Assisted Reading

Morphology

Morphology is the study of the rules that govern how morphemes, the minimal meaningful units of language, are used in a language. Knowledge of morphology helps students spell, decode, and comprehend new words (Collins & Wolter, 2019). It is impossible and unnecessary to explicitly teach every word a child might need to know. In fact, of the 10,000 words a fifth grader will encounter in reading, about 4,000 of them will be derivations of more frequently used words (Kamhi & Catts, 2012). Teaching of morphology can focus on three areas: prefixes, suffixes, and root words.

- Prefixes — these are the easiest to teach because the definitions are consistent and do not change the part of speech as suffixes do (Denton et al., 2007). Additionally, twenty prefixes make up 97% of prefixed words in English (White, Sowell, & Yanagihara, 1989).
- Suffixes — these are more difficult to teach as the definitions are not as consistent or concrete. Stahl (1999) suggests that it is more important for students to have experience with suffixed words versus learning definitions of specific suffixes.
- Roots and Base Words — these contain the basic meaning of the word, and it is important for students to be able to isolate, recognize, and recall the meanings of roots and base words to determine the meaning of complex words (Reading Teacher Sourcebook, 2007). A base word can stand alone (e.g., *depend* in *independent*) and a root cannot (e.g., *cred* in *incredible*).
  - Sample Activities
    - Examples, Nonexamples, and Silly Words
      - Examples (redo, rewrite, replay)
      - Nonexamples (ready, reason, really)
      - Silly words (resleep, redine, reswim)
    - Pocket Charts to Manipulate Words with Varying Morphemes

- Word Trees (prefixes on left, roots and base words in trunk, suffixes on right)
- Frayer Model Chart
- Multiple Opportunities for Practice
  - Vocabulary Lessons
  - Discussion During Reading
  - Modeling and Use of Word Part Strategy
- Word Part Analysis with Word Part Clue Evaluation Chart (Diamond, L. & Gutlohn, L., 2006)
- Flip The Chip
- SLP-Teacher Interprofessional Classroom Morphological Awareness Approach (Collins & Wolter, 2019)

Word Part Clue Evaluation Chart

WORD	No Prefix and Root Word	Prefix and Root Word	Prefix + Root = Meaning	Prefix + Root ≠ Meaning

Semantics

Semantics refers to the meaning of words and combinations of words in a language. If comprehension is the ultimate goal of reading (NICHD, 2000), then it would make sense that the goal of instruction in the area of semantics (and, also, phonemic awareness, fluency, and morphology) is to improve reading comprehension. Students must develop a literate vocabulary—more specific vocabulary and more complex syntactic structures—to develop comprehension skills (Kamhi & Catts, 2012). In fact, Cunningham and Stanovich found that children's vocabulary in kindergarten and first grade is one of the best predictors of their language comprehension skills in middle school (1997).

- Tier 2 Vocabulary — More complex, frequently occurring words; words that students will see and use often in academic settings
- Multiple Meaning Words — Words that have different meanings in different subject areas
- Figurative Language — A form of expression that does not use the strict or realistic meaning of words. Common in comparisons and exaggerations, it's usually used to add a creative flourish to written or spoken language or explain a complicated idea.
- Context clues — Surrounding words or phrases that provide a reader with information about the meaning of unfamiliar words

Guide for Context Clues Practice

Unfamiliar Word	Signal Word or Punctuation	TYPE OF CONTEXT CLUE: Definition, Synonym, Antonym, Example, or General	My Definition

Comprehension

"Good readers must know why they are reading; they must be able to recognize whether they are achieving their goal in reading, and if they are not, they must be able to implement strategies to remediate comprehension difficulties" (Westby, 2014, p. 339). Before, during, and after reading, effective readers automatically utilize strategies to help them understand what they are reading. Most struggling readers, however, do not do this.

Comprehension, the ability to gain meaning from text, is essentially the ultimate goal of reading (RTS, 2007). Struggling readers require direct strategy instruction and sufficient practice in the area of comprehension. Additionally, students with deficits in decoding have also exhibited deficits in executive functioning skills (i.e., working memory, inhibitory control, and cognitive or mental flexibility) and metacognition. (Westby, 2014) Thus, comprehension instruction should focus on strategy instruction as well as developing metacognitive and executive functioning skills.

Is the student a strategic reader? Does the student monitor and self-correct errors? Does he or she stop and form connections to the text?

Sample Activities:

- QAR — *Question Answer Relationship* provides a basis for teaching three comprehension strategies: locating information; showing text structures and how the information is organized; and determining when an inference or reading between the lines is required (T. E. Raphael, 1982; 1986). The following subtypes of questions are targeted:
    - ○ **Right There**: the answer is found in the text, usually as a phrase contained within one sentence.
    - ○ **Think and Search:** the answer is in the text; however, the student is required to combine separate sections or pieces of text to answer the question.

- o ***Author and You:*** the answer is not directly stated in the text, so the student draws on prior knowledge as well as what the author has written to answer the question.
- o ***On Your Own:*** requires students to think about what is already known from their reading and experience (prior knowledge) to formulate an answer.

QAR	
IN THE BOOK	
Right There	**Think and Search**
The answer is in one place in the text. You can put your finger on it! Words from the question and words that answer the questions are often "right there" in the same sentence.	The answer is in several places in the text. You put together (think and search) different parts of the text to find the answer.
• Reread • Scan • Look for keywords.	• Skim or reread • Look for important information • Piece together different parts from the text to answer the question.
IN MY HEAD	
Author and You	**On My Own**
The answer is not in the text.	The answer is not in the
• Think about how what you know and how what's in the text fit together • Reread • Think about what you already know and what the text says • Predict.	text. • Think about what you already know • Think about what you've read before • Make connections.

Source: T. E. Raphael. 1982: 19.

- Think Aloud — A type of modeling in which the SLP verbalizes what he or she is thinking to make the thought process apparent to students. An SLP can model making predictions, describing the pictures they form in their heads about the information, developing analogies, as well as making inferences from pictures and words, and utilizing repair strategies. (Westby, 2014)

- Somebody-Wanted-But-So Strategy — Used during or after reading, it provides a framework to use when summarizing the action of a story by identifying key elements. This strategy also helps students identify the main ideas, recognize cause and effect relationships, generalize, identify similarities and differences between characters, and become aware of various points of view. While it is more often used with narrative text, it can also be used with expository text. (MacOn, Bewell, & Vogt, 1991; Beers, 2003)

Individuals with dyslexia often make spelling errors that are similar to the errors seen in reading. Interventions in spelling (and writing) are not unlike many of the interventions described above. Phonics instruction, instruction of regular spelling patterns (e.g., TCH and DGE are used after short vowels; CH and GE are used after long vowels; patch vs. peach), and analyzing the morphemes in words are just a few ways to address spelling challenges in individuals with dyslexia (Hebert et al., 2018).

In writing, executive functioning involves planning, organizing, setting goals, self-regulating, and self-monitoring. Teaching strategies that focus on language components such as syntax, discourse structure, and the organizational features of text help students compensate for the main difficulty those with dyslexia encounter: spelling. They are then able to focus on higher language skills (Hebert et al., 2018).

Furthermore, Sumner et al. (2016) noted that hesitant spelling affected vocabulary choices when writing. Interventions such as sentence combining, in addition to the morphological and semantic interventions described earlier in the chapter, help children make connections between oral language and writing. Interventions should include addressing a variety of syntactic structures, including use of conjunctions, combining independent and dependent clauses, and using prepositional phrases. Multiple sentence combining exercises can be used to group ideas into paragraphs (Hebert et al., 2018). Lastly, teaching text structures (i.e., narrative, compare and contrast, cause and effect, persuasive writing) helps simplify for students how to organize text related to the purpose of their writing (Hebert et al., 2018).

SOMEBODY
Who is the main character/person?

WANTED
What did the character / person want?

BUT
What was the problem?

SO
How did the character/person try to solve the problem?

THEN
What was the resolution/outcome?

Biography

Christina L. Pompeo, M.S., CCC-SLP, has been a dedicated speech-language pathologist for 25 years in public schools with extensive experience educating students with emotional, behavioral, learning, and communication challenges. She presently works full-time at a fifth/sixth grade school and a lower elementary school in Avon, CT, with experience in grades preschool through twelfth.

During her time in the public schools, Christina has participated in professional development and trainings, both in and out of district, including Social Thinking, Tips and Tools for Effective Supervision, MAPS/PATH, Lindamood-Bell Visualizing and Verbalizing, and Writing Workshop. She has developed and lead pragmatic language/social skills lessons for all general education classrooms, was a member of the Accessible Education Materials (AEM) workgroup, developed and lead professional development sessions for staff, and was invited by the superintendent to be a member of the Social Emotional Learning Workgroup where she helped develop social and emotional learning goals for the district strategic plan for grades kindergarten through high school. Christina is continually cultivating mentoring and leadership skills through continuing education experiences, including graduate-level teaching, clinical supervision, and participation in ASHA's Leadership Development Program-Schools 2019–2020.

Christina is also a course facilitator at Speech@Emerson, Emerson College's online graduate program. At Speech@Emerson, she has facilitated speech sound disorders and language and literacy disabilities, as well as developed, read, and scored child cases for comprehensive exams, been a guest lecturer in comprehensive exam preparatory course office hours for school-age cases prior to comprehensive exams, and served as an immersion facilitator during weekend-long unique academic and clinical learning experiences, including dialogic reading, preschool screening, hearing screening, oral mechanism screening, and exit interviews. Most recently, Christina became the owner of a private practice in Simsbury, CT. Connect by Christina Pompeo, LLC will begin seeing clients during the summer of 2022.

Christina maintains a certificate of clinical competence in speech-language pathology from the American Speech-Language-Hearing Association (ASHA) and is certified through the Connecticut State Department of Education and the Connecticut Department of Public Health. You can find her on Facebook at Connect by Christina Pompeo, LLC, on Instagram @connectbyclp, on Twitter @ChristinaPompeo, and on LinkedIn @christinapompeo.

References

American Speech-Language-Hearing Association. (2001). *Roles and responsibilities of speech-language pathologists with respect to reading and writing in children and adolescents* [Position Statement]. Retrieved from www.asha.org/policy.

Beers, K. (2003). *When kids can't read, what teachers can do: A guide for teachers.* Portsmouth, NH: Heinemann.

Boudreau, D., & Larsen, J. (2004). Contributing our voice: Speech-language pathologists as members of the literacy team. *Perspectives on Language and Learning Education,* 11(3), 8–12.

Collins, G., & Wolter, J. A. (2019). Morphological awareness strategies to promote academic success at tier 1 through interprofessional collaboration. *Perspectives of the ASHA Special Interest Groups, 4,* 781-789.

Cunningham, A. E., & Stanovich, K. E. (1997). Early Reading Acquisition and Its Relation to Reading Experience and Ability 10 Years Later. *Developmental Psychology,* 33, 934-945.

Denton, Carolyn. (2012). Response to intervention for reading difficulties in the primary grades: Some answers and lingering questions. *Journal of learning disabilities.* 45. 232-43. 10.1177/0022219412442155.

Denton, C., Bryan, D., Wexler, J., Reed, D., & Vaughn, S. (2007). *Effective instruction for middle school students with reading difficulties: The reading teacher's sourcebook.* Austin, TX: Vaughn Gross Center for Reading and Language Arts at The University of Texas at Austin.

Diamond, L., & Gutlohn, L. (2006). Teaching vocabulary. Retrieved from http://www.readingrockets.org/article/teaching-vocabulary.com

Eunice Kennedy Shriver National Institute of Child Health and Human Development, NIH, DHHS. (2000). Report of the National Reading Panel: Teaching Children to Read: Reports of the Subgroups (00-4754). Washington, DC: U.S. Government Printing Office.

Hebert, H., Kearns, D., Hayes, J., Bazis, P., & Cooper, S. (2018). Why Children With Dyslexia Struggle With Writing and How to Help Them. *Language, Speech, and Hearing Services in Schools*, 49, 843-863.

Kamhi, A. G., & Catts, H. W. (2012). *Language and reading disabilities* (3rd ed.). Boston, MA: Pearson.

Klingner, J. K., Vaughn, S., Arguelles, M. E., Tejero Hughes, M., & Ahwee Leftwich, S. (2004). Collaborative strategic reading: "Real-world" lessons from classroom teachers. *Remedial and Special Education*, 25(5), 291–302.

MacOn, J., Bewell, D., & Vogt, M. (1991). *Responses to Literature*. Newark, DE: International Reading Association.

Montgomery, J. (2019). The bridge of vocabulary: Evidence-based activities for academic success (2nd ed.). Bloomington, MN: NCS Pearson.

Raphael, T. & Au, K. (2005). *QAR:* Enhancing comprehension and test taking across grades and content areas. *Reading Teacher, 59*, 206-221.

Sanfilippo, J., Ness, M., Petscher, Y., Rappaport, L., Zuckerman, B., Gaab, N. (2020). Reintroducing Dyslexia: Early Identification and Implications for Pediatric Practice. *Pediatrics, 146*, 1.

Scarborough, H. S. (2005). Developmental relationships between language and reading: Reconciling a beautiful hypothesis with some ugly facts. In H. W. Catts & A. G. Kamhi (Eds.), *The connections between language and reading disabilities* (p. 3–24). Lawrence Erlbaum Associates Publishers.

Schuele, C. M., & Boudreau, D. (2008). Phonological awareness intervention: Beyond the basics. *Language, Speech, and Hearing Services in Schools, 39*, 3-20.

Stahl, S. A. (1999). Why Innovations Come and Go (and Mostly Go): The Case of Whole Language. *Educational Researcher, 28*(8), 13–22.

Sumner, E., Connelly, V., & Barnett, A. L. (2016). The Influence of Spelling Ability on Vocabulary Choices When Writing for Children With Dyslexia. *Journal of Learning Disabilities*, 49(3), 293–304.

Vaughn, S. & Linan-Thompson, S. (2004). *Research-based methods of reading instruction*. Alexandria, VA: ASCD.

Wasowicz, J. (2021). A speech-to-print approach to teaching reading. *LDA Bulletin, 5(2)*.

Westby, C. (2014). A language perspective on executive functioning, metacognition, and self-regulation in reading. In C. A. Stone, E. R. Silliman, B. J. Ehren, & G. P. Wallach (Eds.), *Handbook of language and literacy: Development and disorders* (2nd ed.), p. 339-358. New York, NY: Guilford Press.

White, T. G., Sowell, J., & Yanagihara, A. (1989). Teaching elementary students to use word-part clues. *The*

Reading Teacher, 42(4), 302–308. Retrieved from http://www.jstor.org/stable/20200115

Yopp, H. K. (1995). Read-aloud books for developing phonemic awareness: An annotated bibliography. *The Reading Teacher, 48.*

Christina L. Pompeo

Chapter 6
Programs/Curricula

By Jeannette Roberes, M.Ed., M.S., CCC-SLP

"Your character is more important than your credentials."

- Jeannette Roberes

During the early enactment of the Literacy-Based Promotion Act in Mississippi, my knowledge of dyslexia preceded me. Every classroom or therapy setting that I entered became an informal Q&A of sorts. Honestly, being the go-to person for dyslexia intervention came with perks like always having seats saved for me during staff professional development meetings, so my colleagues could pick my brain. It also, however, helped me see the cracks in the education system, not just in how K–12 teachers were prepared but in how the cracks created rifts among the administrators, teachers, therapists, and students alike.

Dyslexia isn't a mandatory prerequisite or corequisite for SLPs, which makes it that much harder to assess, diagnose, treat, and develop intervention plans. For the same reason, when surveyed, 51% of SLPs stated that they were uncomfortable with treating dyslexia and 72% stated that they were unfamiliar with Structured Literacy. These stark statistics came from research we compiled after surveying nearly 90 U.S.-based speech-language pathologists in 2021. Conversely, this data draws me to answer two questions within this chapter:

1. What certificates should SLPs attain to gain more knowledge of dyslexia?
2. Which out-of-the-box literacy programs should SLPs consider using?

Academic Programs and Certificates

When researching a Structured Literacy-based program that is built on the Orton-Gillingham approach for training courses, be sure to look for programs/courses that have been accredited. Some will offer credentials to add to your professional title. The International Multisensory Structured Language Education Council (IMSLEC) holds their accredited courses to rigorous standards that, in turn, allow the courses to certify qualified individuals who meet these standards as teachers, therapists, and instructors. American Speech-Language-Hearing Association's (ASHA) Continuing Education Approved Providers also provide lessons of your choice. Other reliable accreditation programs serving those with dyslexia are found through the Academic Language Therapy Association, the International Dyslexia Association, and the Academy of Orton-Gillingham Practitioners and Educators, also called the Orton-Gillingham Academy.

Multiple collegiate or stand-alone programs also provide training. For instance, the DuBard Association Method® is a professional development program. It is accredited by the International Multisensory Structured Language Education Council (IMSLEC), accredited by the International Dyslexia Association (IDA) for meeting the IDA Knowledge and Practice Standards for Teachers of Reading, and is an American Speech-Language-Hearing Association (ASHA) Continuing Education Approved Provider.

The WRS Level I certified individual is eligible for the Wilson® Dyslexia Practitioner (W.D.P.) credential. This credential recognizes individuals as prepared to diagnostically teach students identified with a language-based learning disability, such as dyslexia, at the beginning levels of encoding and reading.

The Center for Effective Reading Instruction (CERI), an affiliate of the International Dyslexia Association, issues certifications to those who possess the knowledge and skill necessary to implement Structured Literacy practices. Select CERI certifications are awarded only to those therapists who have demonstrated the ability to have a meaningful impact on the rate of improvement for students identified as "at risk" for reading failure or identified with a specific learning disability, including dyslexia. Professionals graduating from an IDA-accredited program are prepared to earn a CERI certification.

A certified academic language therapist (CALT) is a professional credential to describe an individual who has the expertise to provide services to individuals who have difficulty acquiring the basic language skills necessary to read, write, and spell. CALTs have a deep knowledge of the structure of the English language and the experience to apply these skills in creating an individualized plan for the remediation of dyslexia and related learning differences. The CALT credential ensures that an individual has completed a Comprehensive Therapist Level Multisensory Structured Language Training course that is Orton-Gillingham based and accredited by the International Multisensory Structured Language Education Council (IMSLEC). Some of the scripted programs mentioned below provide training and certification to use their programs effectively.

Scripted Programs

Whether a specific Orton-Gillingham reading program will work for the dyslexic students on your caseload depends on each of their specific needs. Therefore, it's good if you pay attention to the details of each program. Notice what kinds of activities each program uses for teaching reading, and see if they are activities that will engage your students. These programs have been compiled from both experience and research that the University of Michigan Dyslexia Help has posted on their website. Each Orton-Gillingham reading program for dyslexia is a little bit different in its teaching. If you know your student's learning style before choosing an Orton-Gillingham reading program, you can choose a program that teaches the way your student learns with a focus on skills that underlie reading.

Depending on the program, it may focus on one or more of the various skills that underlie reading—oral language, phonemic awareness, vocabulary, comprehension, spelling, or writing. In addition, other resources were created using these strategies that can be used to supplement any curriculum, such as Blast Off to Reading and Explode the Code. Alternatively, you could search for Orton-Gillingham resources on the Florida Center for Reading Research (FCRR) resource database to supplement any curriculum. The FCRR Resource Database pulls together over 650 materials from across the center's numerous research, innovation, and engagement activities.

Below is a list of reading programs that incorporate Orton-Gillingham or equivalent approaches, which include emphasis on phonemic awareness, fluency, and strategies for spelling and comprehension. Some were created specifically for dyslexia and are undergirded in the tenets of Structured Literacy (e.g., the Orton-Gillingham approach, multi-sensory approaches). These vary in cost and user-friendliness.

1. All About Learning Press

    All About Reading teaches phonics, decoding, fluency, and comprehension in a fun and engaging way. All About Spelling teaches encoding skills, spelling rules, and multisensory strategies to help students become proficient spellers for life.

2. The Barton Reading & Spelling System

The Barton Reading & Spelling System is a one-on-one tutoring system that improves spelling, reading, and writing skills. It works well for children, teenagers, and adults who struggle due to dyslexia or a learning disability.

3. Equipped for Reading Success

Equipped for Reading Success is a comprehensive step-by-step program that presents more than 20 strategies to improve memory and effortless word retrieval skills to overcome reading difficulties for early level readers.

4. Expanding Expression Tool Kit

This multi-sensory mnemonic strategy facilitates language organization. The kit targets elementary school students, though it can also be used with older students to help with vocabulary, writing, and organization.

5. The Family Fun with Fluency Kit

Produced by the Neuhaus Education Center, this manual contains a set of passages marked at the hundredth word. A student can read the passage to the hundredth word while a therapist notes the duration and tracks progress over time.

6. The Lexia-Herman Method

Composed of three programs, this method encourages improved reading comprehension by targeting basic phonemic awareness through a mix of blending, segmenting, and sound exercises.

7. The Lindamood-Bell LiPS Program

This program encourages phonemic awareness by helping users understand how mouth movements correspond to spoken sounds. Students can then apply this understanding to their speech, spelling, and reading and see improvements.

8. Logic of English (LOE)

LOE Foundations is a complete multi-sensory phonics, reading, handwriting, and spelling program geared for kids ages 4–7. There are 4 levels of Foundations:

- Level A covers basic phonemic awareness for short vowel words.
- Level B covers short sentences, long vowels, schwa sounds, and multi-letter phonograms.
- Level C covers paragraphs, new spelling rules and phonograms, and multi-syllable words.
- Level D masters basic phonograms, deepening spelling skills, and reading children's books.

9. Nessy Reading

Nessy helps students master foundational reading skills. This program is designed to meet the Common Core and most rigorous state standards, the structure is systematic, and data reports are clearly organized and easy to understand.

10. Preventing Academic Failure

Preventing Academic Failure (PAF) is a comprehensive, structured language program for teaching reading, spelling, and handwriting using multisensory techniques. It is an effective beginning reading program for all children. It incorporates instructional practices supported by the latest research and recommended by the National Reading Panel. PAF is the only Orton-Gillingham adapted instruction that is coordinated with a comprehensive reading series and recently authorized by New York City Public Schools.

11. Project Read

Project Read is a language arts curriculum that is carefully designed for all age groups and learning profiles. Piloted in 1969 by Victoria Greene, the Project Read program has helped students in areas of phonics, reading comprehension, and written expression. From its inception, the three guiding principles have been direct instruction of the concepts and skill of language, presentation of concepts and skills in their dependent order (from simplest to most complex), and multisensory strategies and materials created specifically for each concept and skill. Project Read has been proven to help close the learning gap by increasing test scores, meeting state standards, and enriching existing RTI models. In addition to classroom materials, Project Read offers staff development tools for effective intervention in reading and in written and oral language.

12. The RAVE-O Curriculum

This curriculum is designed to improve reading fluency and comprehension of second through fifth graders. Through word play activities, RAVE-O systematically walks students through carefully selected core words at the phonemic, orthographic, semantic, syntactic, and morphological levels.

13. Read Naturally

This program aims to improve reading proficiency through modeling, repetitive reading, and student progress monitoring. It provides students with practice reading and writing problems that help the practitioner gauge progress and set reading fluency goals.

14. Reading Horizons

Reading Horizons products and trainings are powered by a research-based method that clearly explains the structures and patterns of the English language. Instructional software individualizes learning for each student's needs. The software can reinforce instruction or be used as the primary source of instruction.

15. SPELL-Links

SPELL-Links uses a speech-to-print word study approach that leverages the brain's innate, biological wiring and organization for oral language. Unlike other reading programs, which begin with the written letter and teach students to match the letter to a sound, SPELL-Links first helps students learn how to attend to the sound structure of spoken English words and then how to connect and combine sounds (phonology), letter patterns (orthography, mental orthographic images), and meanings (semantics, morphology) to read and spell words.

16. Wilson Reading System

This language-based program teaches the fundamentals of vocabulary and language by giving its users the tools to understand the English language coding system. It utilizes the Orton-Gillingham multi-sensory approach to assist readers.

Research shows that the most effective way to provide intervention to a student with dyslexia is to use a direct intervention program (those listed above) and a computer-based practice program. A child with dyslexia requires 200 to 300, or more, repetitions of practice with each phoneme. By combining the two intervention methods, your student will have ample practice.

Each Orton-Gillingham reading program for dyslexia below is for use with a computer. Some of them are online, so you can use those programs anytime, anywhere. Others you must download to your computer as software.

1.   Fast ForWord Early Literacy

The Fast ForWord program begins with Phonemic Awareness as a starting point. Many parents say it is an excellent program. It has a lot of research behind it. Fast ForWord is one of the top computer-based choices.

2.   HearBuilder

This program focuses on basic concepts, following directions, phonological awareness, auditory memory, and sequencing. HearBuilder also has research to support its effectiveness. The program is priced right for most home users. There are built-in progress reports, so you can know if your student is progressing through the program. Hear Builder is for K–eighth graders. However, I think it would be alright for a high school student who doesn't care what a program looks like. The graphics are not overly babyish, which is a complaint some older students have had about other programs. Overall, HearBuilder would be a good practice program to use daily.

3. Lexia Reading

Lexia meets Common Core standards and has timed drills. The timed items are frustrating to students with a slow processing speed. If the student has a neurologically slow processing speed, then this program isn't likely to be your best fit. Lexia has many different practice activities within the five levels. The program is very thorough. It begins with basic vowel sounds and later teaches roots, prefixes, suffixes, and syllabication. This program is a great teaching tool when used daily.

4. Multisensory Reading, Spelling, and Penmanship

This is a multi-sensory reading, spelling, and penmanship program. It builds relationships between symbols and sounds in the English language. The program uses self-paced repetition. It uses close association of visual, auditory, and kinesthetic items to improve a student's language skills. This program has computer-based and app-based practice. It is a multi-sensory dyslexia program your student can use on the computer. It's best for students who like spending time on the computer.

5. Prolexia Ultra Phonics Tutor

This program is great for practicing handwriting and phonemic awareness together. Learning these skills together streamlines your child's educational day. Using their "light pen" is helpful because it will help your student develop handwriting skills more easily.

Now that you have a glimpse of what exists, I hope you will make a choice that benefits you and your students. As we continue to pursue professional learning opportunities, I know you'll appreciate how your work will evolve. The benefits of dyslexia certifying programs go beyond career advancement. More knowledge in the area of language-based learning disorders can help us redefine our passions and boost our awareness for the benefit of our field. The world of literacy is rapidly changing, and as therapists, we need to advance our skills as we strive for relevant work.

Associations & Programs

All About Learning Press

Equipped for Reading Success

Expanding Expression Tool Kit

Fast ForWord Early Literacy

HearBuilder

Lexia Reading

Logic of English

Multisensory Reading, Spelling, and Penmanship

Nessy Reading

Preventing Academic Failure

Project Read

Prolexia Ultra Phonics Tutor

Read Naturally

Reading Horizons

SPELL-Links

The Academic Language Therapy Association

The Academy of Orton-Gillingham Practitioners

The American Speech-Language-Hearing Association (ASHA)

The Barton Reading & Spelling System

The Center for Effective Reading Instruction (CERI)

The DuBard Association Method®

The Family Fun with Fluency Kit

The Speech-Language Pathologist's Guide to Dyslexia

The International Dyslexia Association

The International Multisensory Structured Language Education Council

The Lexia-Herman Method

The Lindamood-Bell LiPS Program

The Neuhaus Education Center

The RAVE-O Curriculum

The Wilson® Dyslexia Practitioner

Wilson Reading System

Biography

Jeannette Roberes is an author who has worked as a speech-language pathologist, software engineer, and educator. She has spoken in over 40 countries and has earned recognition in *The Washington Post* and *U.S. News & World Report,* among other professional acknowledgements. Jeannette's commitment to life-long learning is noted through her LETRS® early childhood facilitator certification and her Fast ForWord® and PROJECT READ® curriculum certifications. Her debut book, *Technical Difficulties: Why Dyslexic Narratives Matter in Tech*, has received five-star reviews across Goodreads and Amazon. It is available on any online platform where books are sold. Jeannette is the chief academic officer of Bearly Articulating and a board member of Smiles for Speech. When she is not speaking or traveling, you can find her on the following social channels:

Instagram: @bearly_articulating

TikTok: @bearly_articulating

Pinterest: @bearlyarticulating

Twitter: @bearlyartic

Facebook: Bearly Articulating

YouTube: Bearly Articulating

Project Oversight by Jeannette Roberes and Courtney Overton

Biography for Courtney Overton

Courtney Overton, MS, CCC-SLP is a speech-language pathologist and literacy specialist. She is the owner and founder of Speech of Cake, a private practice in Alexandria, Virginia specializing in speech sound disorders and dyslexia. With a passion for shaping future clinicians, Courtney also serves as a clinical fellowship mentor at Speech of Cake, a clinical supervisor at The George Washington University, and an adjunct professor of speech sound disorders at Emerson College. Courtney continues to advocate for neurodivergent students and students of color by providing seminars, workshops, and keynotes on a national level through her organizations, DiverCity SLP and The SLP Guide to Dyslexia.

Courtney is a doctoral candidate in literacy, culture, and language education at Indiana University with a minor in educational leadership. She recently earned a certificate in entrepreneurship from Cornell University. Courtney attended Emerson College in Boston, Mass., to earn a master's degree in speech-language pathology, and she obtained a bachelor's degree in speech-language pathology, minor in linguistics, and certificate in American Sign Language at the University of Pittsburgh in Pittsburgh, Pennsylvania.

Courtney is a member of For(bes) the Culture, National Black Association for Speech-Language and Hearing, American Speech-Language Hearing Association, International Literacy Association, International Dyslexia Association, Pearl and Ivy Educational Foundation, Incorporated, and Alpha Kappa Alpha Sorority, Incorporated.

Courtney is trained in PROMPT, Tethered Oral Tissues (TOTs), Tongue Tips, Thumbs Up!, Story Grammar Marker, Orton-Gillingham, Lindamood Bell, Lucy Calkins, Reading Mastery, Corrective Reading, Read Well, Language!, Wilson, Qualitative Reading Inventory, Dyslexia Fundamentals, The Logic of English, Social Thinking, and Unstuck and On Target. She specializes in evaluating, diagnosing, and treating orofacial myofunctional disorders, articulation disorders, phonological disorders, reading/writing disabilities, language disorders, and social skills.

Follow Courtney on Instagram: @speechofcakeinc, @slpguidetodyslexia, and @divercityslp.

Resources

Assessment Checklist

Areas to be assessed:

Oral Language

_____

Phonological Processing

_____

Vocabulary Knowledge

_____

Word Recognition

_____

Decoding

_____

Spelling

_____

Rapid Automatic Naming

_____

Reading Comprehension

_____

Reading Fluency

_____

Tool/Assessment used:

Dyslexia Goal Bank for SLPs

When writing goals and objectives, think about if the child moved to another district or began working with another SLP. Would the new SLP be able to take your plan and know exactly what to do with it? This doesn't necessarily mean the activities the SLP would use, rather the skill or skills that will be targeted and how (i.e., type and amount of prompting/cueing, support, strategies, etc.). Accuracy criterion and type/amount of prompting will vary based on students, personal preference, and data collection. These are examples that can be easily modified to fit individual needs. The structure/wording of the goals has been changed throughout to offer alternatives to writing them.

Phonemic Awareness

- <u>Blending Sounds into Words:</u>

Given CV (consonant/vowel) and VC (vowel/consonant) word structures (e.g., no, on, so, as, low, all), Student/Child will blend continuant sounds (e.g., f, l, m, n, r, s, v, z) in structured activities with 80% accuracy (or 8/10 times) over 3 sessions with minimal verbal prompting (i.e., 1-2 prompts).

Given CV (consonant/vowel) and VC (vowel/consonant) word structures (e.g., to, at, do, odd, go, egg), Student/Child will blend stop sounds (e.g., p, b, t, d, k, g) in structured activities with 80% accuracy (or 8/10 times) over 3 sessions with minimal verbal prompting (i.e., 1-2 prompts).

Given CVC (consonant/vowel/consonant) word structures (e.g., moon, fish), Student/Child will blend continuant sounds (e.g., f, l, m, n, r, s, v, z) in structured activities with 80% accuracy (or 8/10 times) over 3 sessions with minimal verbal prompting (i.e., 1-2 prompts).

Given CVC (consonant/vowel/consonant) word structures (e.g., cat, fat, dish), Student/Child will blend stop (e.g., p, b, t, d, k, g) and continuant sounds (e.g., f, l, m, n, r, s, v, z) in structured activities with 80% accuracy (or 8/10 times) over 3 sessions with minimal verbal prompting (i.e., 1-2 prompts).

Student/Child will blend sounds in CCVC (consonant/consonant/vowel/consonant) word structures (e.g., small, flag, stop, train) in structured activities with 80% accuracy (or 8/10 times) over 3 sessions with minimal verbal prompting (i.e., 1-2 prompts).

Student/Child will blend sounds in CVCC (consonant/vowel/consonant/consonant) word structures (e.g., help, camp, kind, raft) in structured activities with 80% accuracy (or 8/10 times) over 3 sessions with minimal verbal prompting (i.e., 1-2 prompts).

- <u>Segmenting Sounds in Words:</u>

Student/Child will segment continuant sounds (e.g., f, l, m, n, r, s, v, z) in CV (consonant/vowel) and VC (vowel/consonant) word structures (e.g., no, on, so, as, low, all) in structured activities with 80% accuracy (or 8/10 times) over 3 sessions with minimal verbal prompting (i.e., 1-2 prompts).

Given CV (consonant/vowel) and VC (vowel/consonant) word structures (e.g., to, at, do, odd, go, egg), Student/Child will segment stop sounds (e.g., p, b, t, d, k, g) in structured activities with 80% accuracy (or 8/10 times) over 3 sessions with minimal verbal prompting (i.e., 1-2 prompts).

Student/Child will segment continuant sounds (e.g., f, l, m, n, r, s, v, z) in CVC (consonant/vowel/consonant) word structures (e.g., moon, fish) in structured activities with 80% accuracy (or 8/10 times) over 3 sessions with minimal verbal prompting (i.e., 1-2 prompts).

When presented with CVC (consonant/vowel/consonant) word structures (e.g., cat, fat, dish) in structured activities, Student/Child will segment stop (e.g., p, b, t, d, k, g) and continuant sounds (e.g., f, l, m, n, r, s, v, z) with 80% accuracy (or 8/10 times) over 3 sessions with minimal verbal prompting (i.e., 1-2 prompts).

Student/Child will segment sounds in CCVC (consonant/consonant/vowel/consonant) word structures (e.g., small, flag, stop, train) in structured activities with 80% accuracy (or 8/10 times) over 3 sessions with minimal verbal prompting (i.e., 1-2 prompts).

When presented with CVCC (consonant/vowel/consonant/consonant) word structures (e.g., help, camp, kind, raft) in structured activities,

Student/Child will segment sounds with 80% accuracy (or 8/10 times) over 3 sessions with minimal verbal prompting (i.e., 1-2 prompts).

- <u>Manipulating Sounds in Words:</u>

Student/Child will delete parts of compound words (e.g., "Say hotdog." "Now, say hotdog without hot.") in structured activities with 80% accuracy (or 8/10 times) over 3 sessions with minimal verbal prompting (i.e., 1-2 prompts).

Student/Child will delete the initial sound in varying word structures (e.g., "Say cat." "Now, say cat without the /k/ sound.") in structured activities with 80% accuracy (or 8/10 times) over 3 sessions with minimal verbal prompting (i.e., 1-2 prompts).

Student/Child will delete the final sound in varying word structures (e.g., "Say belt." "Now, say belt without the /t/ sound.") in structured activities with 80% accuracy (or 8/10 times) over 3 sessions with minimal verbal prompting (i.e., 1-2 prompts).

Student/Child will substitute the initial sound in varying word structures (e.g., "Say belt." "Now, say belt with an /m/ sound instead of the /b/ sound.") in structured activities with 80% accuracy (or 8/10 times) over 3 sessions with minimal verbal prompting (i.e., 1-2 prompts).

Student/Child will substitute the final sound in varying word structures (e.g., "Say cat." "Now, say cat with an /m/ sound instead of the /k/ sound.") in structured activities with 80% accuracy (or 8/10 times) over 3 sessions with minimal verbal prompting (i.e., 1-2 prompts).

Fluency

(Adapted from www.learningabledkids.com)

When reading grade level curriculum material aloud, Student/Child will increase oral reading fluency rate from X# words per minute (baseline) to X# words per minute while maintaining 95% accuracy in 3/4 opportunities.

Given an unfamiliar fifth grade text, Student/Child will accurately read passages with expression, increasing oral reading fluency rate from X# words to X# words per minute, in 3/4 opportunities.

Given unfamiliar fifth grade reading material, Student/Child will fluently and accurately read aloud with fewer than 3 errors per 100 words at a rate of:

- 90 words per minute by December
- 110 words per minute by March
- 120 words per minute by June

Morphology

Given direct instruction, modeling, and practice, Student/Child will identify the meaning of the seven most common prefixes (e.g., un-, re-, im-, in-, il-, ir-, dis-) in structured activities with minimal visual and verbal prompting (i.e., 1-2 prompts) 4/5 times over 3 sessions.

Given an assigned prefix and a graphic organizer, Student/Child will identify examples (e.g., redo, rewrite, replay), nonexamples (e.g., ready, reason, really), and silly words (e.g., resleep, redine, reswim) for five clinician-selected prefixes with minimal visual and verbal prompting (i.e., 1-2 prompts) and 80% accuracy.

Student/Child will identify words containing common suffixes (e.g., -s, -es, -ed, -ing, -ly, -er, -or, -tion, -able, -ible) when reading a grade level text with 80% accuracy in 3/4 opportunities.

Given 25 grade-level curriculum vocabulary words, Student/Child will identify prefixes, base/root words, and suffixes with 80% accuracy over 3 sessions.

Semantics

Given an evidence-based vocabulary program, curriculum materials, visual supports, and practice, Student/Child will use 25 new/novel tier 2/academic vocabulary words (within the following topics: synonyms/antonyms, categorization/classification, meaning/usage, word parts, and wordplay) accurately in context with minimal visual and verbal prompting (i.e., 1-2 prompts) in 3/4 opportunities. (Adapted from Montgomery, 2019)

Given direct instruction, modeling, and practice, Student/Child will use 25 new, grade-level multiple meaning words accurately in sentences with minimal visual and verbal prompting (i.e., 1-2 prompts).

Given direct instruction, modeling, and practice, Student/Child will explain the meaning of figurative/non-literal language (e.g., idioms, similes, metaphors) explaining 15 clinician-selected and grade-level appropriate examples of each.

Given direct instruction, modeling, and practice, Student/Child will demonstrate an understanding of nonliteral language (e.g., similes, metaphors, idioms) in context in grade-level curricular materials with minimal visual and verbal prompting (i.e., 1-2 prompts) and 80% accuracy over 3 sessions.

Comprehension

After reading grade-level curriculum material aloud or silently, Student/Child will respond to "Right There" questions (T. E. Raphael, 1982; 1986) given minimal visual and verbal prompting (i.e., 1-2 prompts) 4/5 times over 3 sessions.

After reading grade-level curriculum material aloud or silently, Student/Child will respond to "Think and Search" questions (T. E. Raphael, 1982; 1986) given minimal visual and verbal prompting (i.e., 1-2 prompts) 4/5 times over 3 sessions.

After reading grade-level curriculum material aloud or silently, Student/Child will respond to "Author and You" questions (T. E. Raphael, 1982; 1986) given moderate visual and verbal prompting (i.e., 3-4 prompts) 4/5 times over 3 sessions.

Given grade-level text and a "Somebody-Wanted-But-So" graphic organizer (MacOn, Bewell & Vogt, 1991, Beers, 2003), Student/Child will identify the main idea and cause/effect relationships in the story in 4/5 opportunities over 3 sessions.

Simple View of Reading

A formula introduced by Gough and Tunmer, 1986; Hoover and Gough, 1990

Printed Word Recognition Language

Ability to apply sound-symbol relationships to read words.

 Language Comprehension

Ability to understand spoken language.

Reading to Gain Meaning

Ability to read and obtain meaning from what was read.

SIGNS *of* DYSLEXIA

THE PRESCHOOL YEARS

- Trouble learning common nursery rhymes, such as "Jack and Jill"
- Difficulty learning (and remembering) the names of letters in the alphabet
- Mispronounces familiar words; persistent "baby talk"

KINDERGARTEN & FIRST GRADE

- Reading errors that show no connection to the sounds of the letters on the page
- Does not understand that words come apart
- Does not associate letters with sounds, such as the letter b with the "b" sound
- Strengths: Curiosity, imagination, excellent comprehension of stories read or told to them

SECOND GRADE THROUGH HIGH SCHOOL

- Very slow in acquiring reading skills
- Reading is slow and awkward
- Searches for a specific word and ends up using vague language when speaking
- Poor spelling and messy handwriting
- Strengths: Excels in areas not dependent on reading, such as math, computers and visual arts

YOUNG ADULTS & ADULTS

- Reading still requires great effort and is done at a slow pace
- Rarely reads for pleasure
- Struggles to retrieve words
- Strengths: empathetic, articulate, think outside of the box and see the big picture

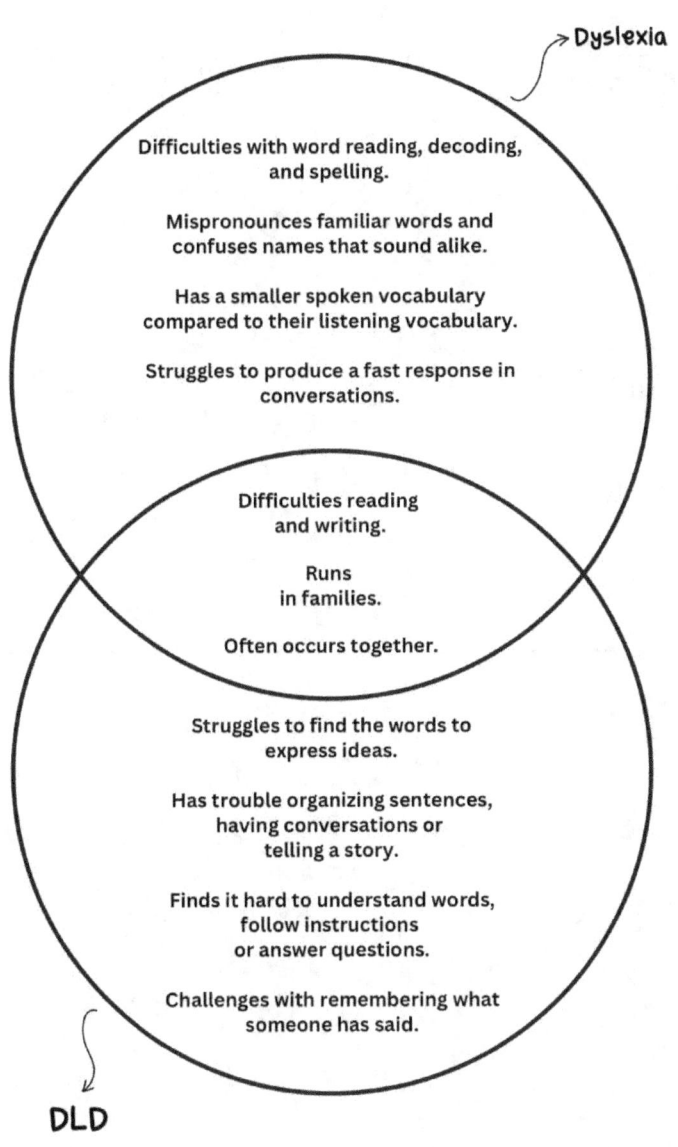

Dyslexia

Difficulties with word reading, decoding, and spelling.

Mispronounces familiar words and confuses names that sound alike.

Has a smaller spoken vocabulary compared to their listening vocabulary.

Struggles to produce a fast response in conversations.

Difficulties reading and writing.

Runs in families.

Often occurs together.

Struggles to find the words to express ideas.

Has trouble organizing sentences, having conversations or telling a story.

Finds it hard to understand words, follow instructions or answer questions.

Challenges with remembering what someone has said.

DLD

Worksheets

Definition	Characteristics
Examples	Non-Examples

Main Idea Form			

Name(s) _____

Date _____

Title or Topic of the Selection

_____

Paragraph	Who or What is the Paragraph About?	Most Important Information About the "Who" or "What"	Key Details

The Vocabulary Strategy

If you read a word that you do not understand:

1) Look for CONTEXT CLUES. Reread the sentence and the surrounding sentences.

2) Can you break the WORD into PARTS? (If not, go to Step 3.)

    a.) Is there a PREFIX? What does it mean?

    b.) Is there a SUFFIX? What does it mean?

    c.) Is there a ROOT WORD? What does it mean?

    d.) Put the meaning of the word parts together. What is the meaning of the whole word?

3.) GUESS what the word means.

4.) INSERT your meaning into the original sentence to see whether it makes sense.

5.) If needed, use the DICTIONARY to confirm your meaning.

The Vocabulary Strategy Worksheet

Word _____

Context
Sentence_____

_____

1. Look for context clues.

    a. Reread the sentence looking for signal words and punctuation.

Signal Words and Punctuation:

    b. Reread the sentences before and after the one with the word in it.

Context Clues:

2. Look for word parts you know. Tell what each word part means.

Prefix:

Suffix:

Root:

Put the parts together. What does this mean?

3. What do you think the word means?

_____

_____

4. Try your meaning in the context sentence. Does it make sense?

_____

5. Check the word with a dictionary if you need to. Remember that many words have more than one meaning, so look for the one that goes with the sentence in the book. Were you right?

_____

Glossary

Balanced Literacy: "A 'philosophical orientation that assumes that reading and writing achievement are developed through instruction and support in multiple environments using various approaches that differ by level of teacher support and child control' (Fountas & Pinnell, 1996). Although phonics, decoding, and spelling may be taught in word study lessons, the skills typically are not emphasized and rarely taught systematically (Spear-Swearling, 2019). Rather, students are encouraged to use word analogies and pictures or context to identify words. Balanced Literacy instruction is focused on shared reading (e.g., the teacher reads aloud to students and asks questions about the text), guided reading (e.g., students read texts at their current ability level and discuss them with the teacher in homogeneous groups), and independent reading (e.g., students self-select books to read on their own)." *—definition from Iowa Reading Research Center*

Certified Academic Language Therapist (CALT): Provides diagnostic, explicit, systematic Multisensory Structured Language intervention, which builds a high degree of accuracy, knowledge, and independence for students with written-language disorders, including dyslexia. CALTs are certified through The Academic Language Therapy Association.

Clinical Psychologist: An individual who studies and implements an integration of science, theory, and clinical knowledge for the purpose of understanding, preventing, and relieving psychologically based distress or dysfunction and to promote subjective well-being and personal development.

Comprehension: The ability to understand what is read—the ultimate goal of reading

Context Clues: Surrounding words or phrases that provide a reader with information about the meaning of unfamiliar words

Decoding: "The ability to apply your knowledge of letter-sound relationships, including knowledge of letter patterns, to correctly pronounce written words. Understanding these relationships gives children the ability to recognize familiar words quickly and to figure out words they haven't seen before." - *definition from Reading Rockets*

Dyslexia: "A Specific Learning Disability that is neurobiological in origin. It is characterized by difficulties with accurate and/or fluent word recognition and by poor spelling and decoding abilities. These difficulties typically result from a deficit in the phonological component of language that is often unexpected in relation to other cognitive abilities and the provision of effective classroom instruction. Secondary consequences may include problems in reading comprehension and reduced reading experience that can impede growth of vocabulary and background knowledge." *-definition from International Dyslexia Association (IDA) Board of Directors*

Educational Diagnostician: Type of special education professional who assesses, diagnoses, and works with children with learning difficulties. These professionals may operate under other titles. They may be called a "learning consultant" or "learning disabilities teacher," but their duties are similar. They work as part of a team of administrators to advise and determine appropriate learning strategies for struggling learners. They may also conduct and interpret assessments within their respective school systems.

Figurative Language: A form of expression that does not use the strict or realistic meaning of words. Common in comparisons and exaggerations, it is usually used to add a creative flourish to written or spoken language or explain a complicated idea.

Fluency: The ability to read text quickly, accurately, and with expression

Functional Magnetic Resonance Imaging (fMRI): "The activity of the neurons constantly fluctuates as you engage in different activities, from simple tasks like controlling your hand to reach out and pick up a cup of coffee to complex cognitive activities like understanding language in a conversation. The brain also has many specialized parts, so activities involving vision, hearing, touch, language, memory, etc. have different patterns of activity. Functional magnetic resonance imaging is a technique for measuring and mapping brain activity that is noninvasive and safe. It is being used in many studies to better understand how the healthy brain works, and in a growing number of studies it is being applied to understand how that normal function is disrupted in disease." - *definition from UC San Diego School of Medicine, Center for Functional MRI*

Literacy-Based Promotion Act (LBPA): Places an emphasis on grade-level reading skills, particularly as students' progress through grades K–3. A student scoring at the lowest achievement level in reading on the established statewide assessment for third grade will not be promoted to fourth grade unless the student qualifies for a good cause exemption.

Metacognition: Awareness and understanding of one's own thought processes

Morphology: The study of the rules that govern how morphemes, the minimal meaningful units of language, are used in a language

Multiple Meaning Words: Words that have different meanings in different subject areas

Neuropsychologist: A person who conducts evaluations to characterize behavioral and cognitive changes resulting from central nervous system disease or injury, such as Parkinson's disease or another movement disorder

Phonemic Awareness: A type of phonological awareness; the ability to hear and manipulate sounds within words, usually demonstrated by segmenting words into their individual sounds and blending sounds to form words; an auditory skill, but should be linked with instruction in letters or letter sounds (phonics)

Phonological Awareness: The awareness of sounds in language

Phonological Memory: Memory for the speech sounds in words, i.e., letter names, names of numbers

Phonological Processing: "The ability to quickly and correctly hear, store, recall, and make different speech sounds." - *definition from National Center on Improving Literacy (NCIL)*

Phonological Production: The ability to produce more phonologically complex or multisyllabic words, i.e., how Danelle's husband has difficulty sequencing the syllables and saying the word "obnoxious"

Phonological Retrieval: Word and name retrieval

Response to Intervention (RTI): An approach that schools use to help all students, including struggling learners. Schools may choose to use an RTI process as one of a variety of measures for evaluating students for learning disability eligibility. RTI is also a way to address behavioral concerns.

Science of Reading: "A vast, interdisciplinary body of scientifically based research about reading and issues related to reading and writing. This research has been conducted over the last five decades across the world, and it is derived from thousands of studies conducted in multiple languages. The science of reading has culminated in a preponderance of evidence to inform how proficient reading and writing develop, why some have difficulty, and how we can most effectively assess, teach, and therefore, improve student outcomes through prevention of and intervention for reading difficulties. The science of reading is derived from research from multiple fields: cognitive psychology, communication sciences, developmental psychology, education, special education, implementation science, linguistics, and neuroscience." - *definition from The Reading League, The Science of Reading: A Defining Movement*

Semantics: Refers to the meaning of words and combinations of words in a language

Specific Learning Disability: "A disorder in one or more of the basic psychological processes involved in understanding or in using language, spoken or written, that may manifest itself in the imperfect ability to listen, think, speak, read, write, spell, or do mathematical calculations, including conditions such as perceptual disabilities, brain injury, minimal brain dysfunction, dyslexia, and developmental aphasia.

"Disorders not included—Specific Learning Disability does not include learning problems that are primarily the result of visual, hearing, or motor disabilities, of intellectual disability, of emotional disturbance, or of environmental, cultural, or economic disadvantage." - *definition from Individuals with Disabilities Education Act (IDEA) Sec. 300.8 (c)(10)*

Structured Literacy: "Highly explicit and systematic teaching of all important components of literacy. These components include both foundational skills (e.g., decoding, spelling) and higher-level literacy skills (e.g., reading comprehension, written expression). Structured Literacy also emphasizes oral language abilities essential to literacy development, including phonemic awareness, sensitivity to speech sounds in oral language, and the ability to manipulate those sounds." - *definition from International Dyslexia Association (IDA)*

Think-Aloud: A type of modeling in which the teacher verbalizes what he or she is thinking to make the thought process apparent to students

Tier 2 Vocabulary: High-frequency words for mature language users and thus instruction in these words can add productively to an individual's language ability. More complex, frequently occurring words; words that students will see and use often in academic settings.

Whole Language: "A method of teaching reading and writing that emphasizes learning whole words and phrases by encountering them in meaningful contexts rather than by phonics exercises." - *definition from Merriam-Webster*